Being United Methodist Christians

Living a Life of Grace *and* Hope

ANDY LANGFORD
ANN LANGFORD DUNCAN
SALLY LANGFORD

Preface by Will Willimon

Abingdon Press
Nashville

BEING UNITED METHODIST CHRISTIANS
LIVING A LIFE OF GRACE AND HOPE

This book is printed on acid-free paper

ISBN: 9781791032142
Library of Congress Control Number: 2023941952

Other Resources to Support This Study

- Six video introductions to the six sections of this book by Ann Langford Duncan. These short, personal, informal, and invitational presentations introduce persons to the theme of each section. Available with a subscription at AmplifyMedia.com.

- Sermon, Worship, and Study Series Download, 9781791032166: Includes suggestions for using this book in worship and preaching. These ideas are useful for clergy and worship planners to spur imaginations in worship, sermons, visuals, and song. Also includes a study guide for small-group study, which offers an outline of the themes from this book for leaders to follow. Available at Cokesbury.com.

MANUFACTURED IN THE UNITED STATES OF AMERICA

DEDICATION

This book was inspired by the work of The Reverend Dr. Thomas A. Langford, Jr. (1929-2000), father, father-in-law, and grandfather. He was a United Methodist pastor, author, theologian, and historian at Duke University for over forty years. He was on the Board of Directors of the definitive *The Works of John Wesley* (Abingdon, 1984-2000). He wrote "Grace Upon Grace: The Mission Statement of The United Methodist Church," adopted in 1988 by the General Conference and recommended anew by the 1999 Council of Bishops, which focuses on the centrality of grace in United Methodist theology and practice. This statement continues to spur global conversation about the mission of The United Methodist Church.

Some of Dr. Langford's books include: *Practical Divinity: Theology in the Wesleyan Tradition* (Abingdon, 1983, revised into two volumes in 1984); *Wesleyan Theology: A Sourcebook* (Labyrinth, 1984); *Grace Upon Grace: The Mission Statement of The United Methodist Church* (Graded Press, 1990); *Doctrine and Theology in The United Methodist Church* (editor, Abingdon, 1991); and *God Made Known* (Abingdon, 1992). At his retirement, he was recognized in *Grace Upon Grace: Essays in Honor of Thomas A. Langford* (Abingdon, 1999).

Thanks to everyone who reviewed, evaluated, and offered revisions to this book, including United Methodist pastors Tom Latimer, Savannah Glover, Mark King, Luke Edwards, David Scott, Fred Jordan; United Methodist Publishing House President Emeritus Neil Alexander; plus members of Central United Methodist Church (Concord, North Carolina) and Burlingame United Methodist Church (Burlingame, California).

CONTENTS

Being a United Methodist Christian has been a challenge in the last couple of years. While most of us were busy being church, a number of fellow Methodists announced that they had had it with The United Methodist Church, that they could no longer be church with people like us, and left. The spectacle of "disaffiliation" has been particularly painful for those of us entrusted with stewardship of a church that we had inherited from generations of faithful Wesleyans.

I have heard that "We need someone to stand up and defend our church." In my teaching, writing, speaking, and preaching, I hope to reinvigorate those who remain committed to the rigorous demands and the peculiar joys of the Wesleyan way of walking with Jesus. My book *Don't Look Back: Methodist Hope for What Comes Next* (Abingdon, 2022) is one of my responses.

Dear faithful, non-separating, non-litigating, but frustrated United Methodists, here's the book you've been needing to celebrate our church. *Being United Methodist Christians* is the gift of two generations of three experienced pastoral leaders who have given us hopeful, biblical, and practical affirmation of the church dreamed by John Wesley.

First Peter 3:15 enjoins followers of Jesus. "Whenever anyone asks you to speak of your hope, be ready to defend it." This book does just that. Pastors Sally, Andy, and Ann affirm the good name and the bright future of The UMC without defensiveness and without misrepresentations of our church.

Sally, Andy, and Ann, all experienced pastors, ministry innovators, denominational leaders, and progeny of the great Methodist theologian Thomas Langford, contend for United Methodist faith and practice without contentiousness. They defend our church and what our church taught us to believe about Jesus by sharing what they love about Wesleyanism, allowing the tradition to speak for itself.

Deftly performing a ministry of encouragement, they give us just what we need to regain confidence that the vision cast by John Wesley's preaching and the passion of Francis Asbury's circuit riders continues to be God's great gift to a world that hasn't yet received the good news of Christ.

With these three pastors guiding us, this period of United Methodist division can be transformed by the Holy Spirit into a time of rebirth and renewal. We need to spend time asking questions like, "What's there about Wesleyan Christianity that made this church particularly helpful to you in your discipleship?" and "Was there one thing that the United Methodists taught you about Jesus that made a difference in your life?" In the middle of all the attacks upon our church, it's time to talk about what's right with The United Methodist Church.

If you're a pastor, wondering how to lead the church in the present moment, or just an average church member attempting to stay in love with and to perform ministry for Christ through The United Methodist Church, you'll love this book.

—United Methodist Bishop Will Willimon

In 1784, John Wesley gathered three Anglican clergy in Bristol, England, and sent them to North America to share the gospel of Jesus Christ. Empowering them with a passion for evangelism, rules for holy living, a list of theological affirmations, and a prayer book entitled *The Sunday Service of the Methodists in North America*, Wesley charged Thomas Coke, Richard Whatcoat, and Thomas Vasey to journey to the brand-new and unchurched United States of America. Kenneth Wyatt captured Wesley's commission in a 1984 painting entitled *Offer Them Christ.*

Several months later, in Baltimore, Maryland, Coke, Whatcoat, and Vasey ordained thirteen additional clergy and consecrated two bishops to form The Methodist Episcopal Church. The new denomination was the first to have the name *Methodist* and the first indigenous denomination in the newly forming United States of America. A flame that began in a rural English parish expanded to a Bible study at Oxford, jumped to a small meeting house in London, crossed the Atlantic Ocean, reached across the North American continent, and spread like wildfire across the world. Today over eighty million people in a variety of denominations across our planet are the spiritual heirs of John Wesley.

Over thirteen million followers of John Wesley now call themselves United Methodist Christians. Most of the persons reading this book have taken holy vows to be part of this denomination or are considering making such a public affirmation of faith. When one joins a local congregation, a person not only professes that Jesus is Savior, but also vows to participate faithfully in the ministries of The United Methodist Church by prayers, presence, gifts, service, and witness.[1] This book helps its readers

3

understand the history, theology, and expectations behind such vows. We believe that the more one knows about The United Methodist Church, the prouder and more hopeful we can all be to be called United Methodist Christians.

Over the past few years, some critics and media outlets have proclaimed the death of The United Methodist Church. Nothing could be further from the truth. We are still the largest traditional Protestant denomination in the United States with congregations in every state and over forty-five nations. New people are responding every day to the United Methodist proclamation of God's grace.

United Methodists still offer Jesus Christ to women, children, and men everywhere. In a thriving congregation established by Filipino United Methodists in the United Arab Emirates, a small Appalachian chapel, a storefront church on top of a trash dump in Manila, a great university in Zimbabwe, a small chapel on Wall Street in New York City, local churches in the Silicon Valley of California, a mega-church in Dallas, congregations in Ukraine and Norway, and around 40,000 other congregations around the world, the flame continues to burn. We are all United Methodists!

Our Council of Bishops, in a 2021 letter to the denomination, described us this way:

> United Methodists all over the globe are liturgical, contemporary, charismatic, social activists, urban, suburban, small town, rural and much more. We are children, youth, young adults, senior adults, new Christians, and mature Christians. We are present on four continents, in more than 45 countries, and we comprise an unknown number of cultures and languages. We are a holy communion of different races, ethnicities, cultures, and perspectives united by the Holy Spirit, driven by the mission of Christ, and bearing the good news of an unmerited grace that changes lives and transforms communities.[2]

How can we describe United Methodists? Where do we come from? What do we believe? How do United Methodists behave?

What are our distinctive characteristics? What is required to be a member of our denomination? How do we grow as disciples of Jesus Christ within this great communion?

In this resource, we offer answers to these questions and others in broad, impressionistic strokes as we describe The United Methodist Church. We introduce how United Methodists think and live as followers of Jesus Christ.

Some of you, like Ann and Andy, have been members of The United Methodist Church since birth. Others of you, like Sally, joined our denomination because of its theology and mission. Many of you are current members but want to know more about who we United Methodists are.

Others of you are new to United Methodism. You may have grown up in another faith tradition or come to this study without any religious background at all. You may have married into this denomination or are looking for a place of worship and service where every member of your family can find a home. You may be here because of a life-altering change—the death of a loved one, a move to a new town, or the religious questions of your child that you cannot answer. You may live in the Philippines, Fiji, Austria, the Democratic Republic of Congo, or the United States.

The United Methodist Church possesses characteristics of many other Christian traditions but has its own distinctive profile. Above all else, United Methodists preach, teach, and live out God's grace. Our denomination also combines knowledge and vital piety, believing that serious theological reflection and vital spiritual practices are both part of the Christian life. United Methodists link personal and social holiness, expecting high personal integrity and deep commitment to social justice. We are both evangelical and sacramental, showing passion for people who have not yet accepted Jesus Christ as Savior and honoring the transforming power of baptism and Holy Communion. We include both strong traditionalists and persistent progressives, welcoming people with many different theological perspectives. Finally, United Methodists are both local and connectional, expressing our faith in local congregations, regional associations, and global missions, so that we might do more together than any of us could do separately.

We—Ann, Sally, and Andy—are proud to be United Methodists. Andy's family has been Methodist for over 175 years. Andy owns an 1866 Methodist hymnal in German, which belonged to his great-great-grandmother in Indiana.[3] Sally grew up in a Southern Baptist congregation but then joined Colliers United Methodist Church where she served as a summer ministerial intern. Ann, the older daughter of this United Methodist clergy couple, is a third-generation United Methodist pastor. Her faith journey has led her from North Carolina to Boston to Togo, West Africa, to mountain congregations in North Carolina, to the Silicon Valley of California. Together, we have been ordained United Methodist pastors for over one hundred years!

The three of us have seen this denomination from many angles. Sally and Andy have served together a seven-congregation parish in the North Carolina mountains, a mill-town congregation, and a large membership church in Charlotte. Sally then became a supervisor of pastors, while Andy served a local congregation. They have visited United Methodist congregations and missions throughout the United States and on three continents. Ann, a Peace Corps veteran, has served several small-town congregations and now pastors a congregation just south of San Francisco that includes persons from over a dozen nations. Most of the illustrations in this book reflect what we have personally witnessed.

Our denomination has blessed the three of us in many ways. The United Methodist Church has paid our salaries, provided parsonages for our housing, nurtured our children, and introduced us to Christians around the world. Most importantly, this denomination has shaped our spiritual formation as disciples of Jesus Christ. The three of us and our families are who we are because of The United Methodist Church.

The three of us have used the outline and contents of this book in Sunday school classes and in sermon series. Pastors may consider using this book as part of an introduction to United Methodism for prospective members and/or a preaching series and/or a congregation-wide study of who we all are as United Methodists.

Over the entrance to Central United Methodist Church in Concord, North Carolina, stands a stained glass window, created in Philadelphia with inch-thick glass and covered with gold leaf. As one enters the sanctuary, the window's title is "Come to Me." Along with a Bible and baptismal shell, Jesus stands with his arms open welcoming a child, an older adult, a person on crutches, a scholar with a book, and others. All are welcome. As one leaves the sanctuary, the window proclaims "Go to All the World." Jesus stands on top of the world with his arms offering a benediction and depicting ships sailing to the four corners of the earth. Go serve everyone. This window captures our United Methodist ethos.

We invite you to claim for yourself the continuing story of God's mighty acts of creation, redemption, and power through Jesus Christ within our great denomination. As you begin or continue to see yourself within this living, dynamic part of the universal body of Jesus Christ, we invite you to live and grow as a United Methodist Christian.

As Thomas Bickerton, the 2023 president of our Council of Bishops, wrote, it is time for our denomination to "Reclaim. Revive. Renew."[4] Let us reclaim who we are, revive our spirits, and renew this wonderful communion.

Hymn Stanzas

O for a thousand tongues to sing
    my great Redeemer's praise,
the glories of my God and King,
    the triumphs of his grace!

My gracious Master and my God,
    assist me to proclaim,
to spread through all the earth abroad
    the honors of thy name.

—Charles Wesley (*The United Methodist Hymnal*, 58)

Other Resources to Support This Study

In addition to this book, The United Methodist Publishing House also provides more help to pastors and leaders to share these core affirmations with other people. These supplemental resources include:

- Six video introductions to the six sections of this book by Ann Langford Duncan. These short, personal, informal, and invitational presentations introduce persons to the theme of each section. Available with a subscription at AmplifyMedia.com.
- Sermon, Worship, and Study Series Download, 9781791032166: Includes suggestions for using this book in worship and preaching. These ideas are useful for clergy and worship planners to spur imaginations in worship, sermons, visuals, and song. Also includes a study guide for small-group study, which offers an outline of the themes from this book for leaders to follow. Available at Cokesbury.com.

Notes

1. *The United Methodist Hymnal*, p. 38, revised by the 2008 General Conference to include "witness."
2. "A Narrative for the Continuing United Methodist Church" (November 2021).
3. 1866 *Deutsches Gersangbuch ver Bisch Methodisten-Kirche, The Little German Hymnal of the Methodist Church*, belonging to Mary Koerner.
4. Bickerton, Tom, "Reclaim. Revive. Renew.: Mid-Term State of The United Methodist Church Address," March 2, 2023; https://www.umc.org/en/content/reclaim-revive-renew-the-necessity-of-union-among-us#transcript.

1. What Is
Our Biblical Story?

United Methodist Christians affirm that the Holy Scriptures contain all things necessary for salvation and are the primary source for Christian doctrine.[1]

Every scripture is inspired by God and is useful for teaching, for showing mistakes, for correcting, and for training character, so that the person who belongs to God can be equipped to do everything that is good.

2 TIMOTHY 3:16-17

The Bible Moths

In 1729, three young adults at Oxford University gathered together in a dorm room to read the Bible. These seekers then invited a twenty-six-year-old professor and newly ordained priest in the Church of England to lead their study for the next six years. The bright, intense scholar was John Wesley. Around the raucous university town, other students called the group "Bible Moths," because like moths around a flame they hovered over the Scriptures. Another name, based on their methodical pattern of biblical study, prayer, fasting, and service, stuck: "Methodists."

Fourteen years later, after thousands of other people around England began to adopt for themselves the devotion of those young men, John Wesley wrote a pamphlet entitled "The Character of a Methodist," in which he described the Methodists:

9

The distinguishing marks of Methodists are not their opinions of any sort. Their assenting to this or that scheme of religion, embracing any particular set of notions, espousing the judgment of one person or of another, are all quite wide of the point. . . . We believe the written word of God to be the only and sufficient rule both of Christian faith and practice.[2]

Wesley did not begin his ministry to create something unique. He neither advocated a peculiar way of being Christian nor intended to form a new Christian denomination. Wesley simply read the Bible and responded to what God commanded. Nevertheless, that gathering of young adults, who studied the Bible and walked in the footsteps of Jesus, marked the beginning of a religious movement that has changed millions of lives and transformed our world in significant ways.

What was or is the role of the Bible in your own spiritual journey?

People of the Book

United Methodists are first and foremost people who read the Bible and seek to be disciples of Jesus Christ. Wesley first learned the stories of Jesus when his mother taught him to read using the Bible. From an early age, Wesley sought to put Jesus's teachings into practice. As an Anglican priest, he preached in the English colony of Georgia and throughout England, Wales, and Ireland. People responded. In 1766, Barbara Heck, a Methodist laywoman in New York City, invited English immigrants and African slaves to her cottage to read the Bible. The movement we know now as The United Methodist Church grew.

As young children, the three of us each learned Bible stories and were given our own copies of the Bible. Sally participated as a youth in Bible drills in her Baptist congregation and later studied Greek and Hebrew to read the Bible in its original languages. All three of us majored in religion in college and took many classes on the Bible. When a college freshman, Ann spent a summer on a Holy Land archaeological dig in Sepphoris, an ancient Roman city just outside Jesus's hometown of Nazareth. We have always viewed our own lives through the biblical stories.

This tradition of Bible study and faithful discipleship continues throughout The United Methodist Church. In the Philippines, while some United Methodists gather in traditional church sanctuaries, other Filipinos gather on top of a large trash dump in Manila to read the Bible. Other United Methodists from the Pacific Islands to Africa to Europe to the United States to Southeast Asia gather in churches, homes, businesses, and parks to read the Bible. Together we listen to God's Word and seek to do God's will.

What memories do you have about the Bible from your childhood or youth as you were growing up? How many Bibles do you own? How often do you read the Bible?

What Is the Bible?

United Methodists believe that the Bible is the primary source for listening to God. The Bible contains sixty-six different books, which were compiled over a thousand years but reflect events over a much longer period of time. Composed by many authors, the books of the Bible spoke to specific audiences in particular historical contexts addressing many different issues.

The human experiences depicted throughout the pages of the Bible are down-to-earth. People are born, marry, have children, get sick, and die. These biblical characters also betray their friends, commit violent acts, and put their own interests before the needs of other people. Yet, throughout the Bible, God reaches out and changes lives. God's Spirit inspired the Bible's authors as they compiled stories of God's mighty acts and celebrated people who became obedient to God.

God's Spirit continues to move within United Methodists today whenever we read the Bible. When we allow the Holy Spirit to inform our reading and hearing of the Bible, then the ancient Scriptures confront us once more with God's life-changing Word.

When has God spoken to you as you read or listened to the words of the Bible?

What Does the Bible Teach?

From Genesis, the first book of the Bible, to the last book, Revelation, God is revealed as our Creator, Redeemer, and Sustainer. At Creation, God formed human beings in the image of God and breathed life into them. God placed humans in a beautiful world and called them into a covenant relationship with God. Over and over again, however, prideful people failed to love God. God cast humans out of Eden and allowed men and women to create their own culture of murder, idolatry, and immorality.

In response, rather than abandoning people as they had abandoned God, God continued to invite persons back into a right relationship with God and other people. Abraham and Sarah were called to leave their native country, travel to a new land, and become a blessing to all peoples. When God's people were slaves in Egypt, God sent Moses to set them free and lead them again to the Promised Land. Spirit-filled men and women served God's people as they crossed the Jordan River into the Promised Land. God granted the people's wish for rulers such as David to establish an earthly kingdom. When the kings ruled unjustly, prophets arose to proclaim God's words of judgment and hope.

In the fullness of time, God sent Jesus Christ, born of Mary and the Holy Spirit. Jesus healed the sick, preached forgiveness and reconciliation, and proclaimed a new reign of God. Jesus called together diverse people of various social, national, and economic backgrounds. When Jesus's ministry was rejected by the religious leaders and Roman officials, he was arrested and crucified.

At its climax, the Bible proclaims that God raised Jesus from the dead. When Jesus the Christ ascended into heaven, the Holy Spirit became the guide and companion for his followers. Through the Holy Spirit, the church was formed, and its members shared with family, friends, and strangers the good news of life redeemed, abundant, and everlasting. Through the witness of Paul, Lydia, and others, the church spread from Jerusalem to Rome to the ends of the earth.

The Bible closes with the hope-filled vision of a new heaven and a new earth as God in Christ brings to fulfillment God's reign of peace and justice. At the end of history and in a new creation, all of God's people will live in harmony with God. United Methodists, along with Christians everywhere, proclaim these core scriptural truths.

What is your favorite story from the Bible?

How Do United Methodists Encounter God through the Bible?

Engaging stories fill the Bible, such as tales of Noah and the ark, Esther and her cousin Mordecai, and Jesus's feeding of 5,000 people with five loaves of bread and two fish. The Bible shares ancient legal codes, beautiful poetry, hymns, and the early history of Judaism and Christianity. And when United Methodists read the Bible, they can expect an encounter with the living God.

United Methodists do not regard the Bible as without error in regard to history or science. The Bible does provide, however, a trust-worthy road map and compass, inviting us to discover in its pages an intimate relationship with Jesus Christ. Everything we need to know about God we discover within the Bible.

Wesley always proclaimed that he was a "person of one book"—the Bible.[3] According to Wesley, God reveals through the biblical story the way to heaven. More than a place of eternal bliss, heaven is also a restored relationship with God and all of God's creation that begins now and lasts forever.[4] United Methodists affirm that "the Holy Scripture containeth all things necessary to salvation"[5] and are "the primary source and criterion for Christian doctrine."[6]

How do you believe the Bible is true?

Listening to the Bible

How can United Methodists hear God's Word in the Bible today? Reading the Bible can be intimidating to anyone when she or he first opens its pages. Some readers begin with one of the four Gospels, perhaps The Gospel According to Mark. Other readers turn to a devotional guide to chart a way through the Bible.

While we may read the Bible alone, our own individual insights are often not enough to fully understand God's Word. We can hear God more clearly when we read the Scriptures with other believers. The New Testament Book of Acts 8:26-40 tells of the disciple Philip's encounter with an Ethiopian official, who was reading aloud the prophet Isaiah. "Do you understand what you are reading?" Philip asked. "How can I," the Ethiopian replied, "unless someone guides me?" Philip sat beside the official and explained the Scripture. As Philip told the Ethiopian about God's love revealed in the life, death, and resurrection of Jesus, the official's life was changed, and he was baptized that very day.

United Methodists still read the Bible together and listen for insights from one another. In small groups in a classroom, a friend's home, or a coffee shop, we read the Bible together and listen for a word from God. Andy's congregation hosted a Bible study at a local pub called The George Washington Tavern. Over coffee and cold drinks, a group of adults read Scripture, asked profound questions of one another, and discovered new relationships with each other and Jesus Christ. Ann and her congregation invite members and friends to grow closer to God and one another through online Bible studies.

Reading the Bible is also central to United Methodist worship. Although United Methodists were leaders in the development of the recent Common English Bible translation used in this book, even so, we United Methodists do not read only one translation of the Bible to the exclusion of others.[7] Because ours is a worldwide denomination, United Methodists read the Bible in many different translations and hundreds of languages. At Shiprock United Methodist Church in the Four Corners area of New Mexico, members hear the Bible read in both Navajo and English. Many predominantly Hispanic, Korean, and Hmong congregations read the Bible in their own languages. In worship, United Methodists often recite or sing the psalms. All of our hymns and contemporary praise choruses are based on Scripture.

All United Methodist pastors use the Bible for their preaching, although in different ways. We celebrate that diversity. Some preachers design their preaching and worship around the Revised Common Lectionary, a three-year sequence of biblical lessons used by many Christians around the world.[8] Other pastors preach through a whole book of the Bible, while still other preachers choose topical themes. Ann has twice preached through the Bible in a year. One of the critical aspects of United Methodist preaching is freedom of the pulpit. Because United Methodist clergy are appointed by a bishop to a congregation, pastors are free to speak the truth in love without fear of a negative congregational reaction that may result in losing a job.

John Wesley often ended his sermons asking, "What say you to this?" The aim of preaching is not to teach a lesson nor tell a nice Bible story nor discuss a topic from the news. Instead, the goal of preaching is to invite all persons to listen for God's voice in a particular passage of the Bible and discern God's call for them and their communities. At our best, United Methodists end their sermons asking "So what? What did you hear? How will you respond?"

Where do you read the Bible or hear the Bible read?

The Bible and the Wesleyan Quadrilateral

Distinctive to our tradition, United Methodists read and interpret the Bible in the context of the traditions of the church, in light of human experiences, and with the use of reason. United Methodists have called this model of theological reflection and interpretation the quadrilateral. The quadrilateral is a four-part dynamic construct of interrelated perspectives; our United Methodist beliefs are grounded in Scripture, informed by Christian tradition, enlivened by multiple human experiences, and tested by informed reason.[9]

We begin by affirming that the Bible, the first side of the quadrilateral, is the primary foundation of our understanding of the Christian faith. The Old and New Testaments are the unique and authoritative standards for Christian doctrine. Wesley sometimes referred to Methodism as "Scriptural Christianity."[10] After studying Scripture, United Methodists then develop theology. Yet, we do not study the Bible within a vacuum.

Tradition is the first filter through which we approach the Bible. Because Christians throughout the ages and in many places have read and reflected on the Bible, United Methodists do not read the Bible starting from scratch. We know the importance of drawing on the knowledge of other interpreters to understand God's living Word. Our tradition includes Wesley's "Notes upon the New Testament," our Methodist "Articles of Religion," and our Evangelical United Brethren "Confession of Faith."[11]

17

A generation ago, Andy's father, to whom this book is dedicated, studied hundreds of Methodist theologians over the past two hundred years within the global Methodist connection. What he discovered, despite the wide diversity of perspectives, was that they all focused on God's grace through Jesus Christ. We continue to learn from these Methodist theologians. In addition, United Methodists have the collective wisdom of theologians and scholars from many diverse Christian communions and other cultures, both past and present. These Christian scholars read the Bible with differing perspectives and help us broaden our understanding of God's Word.

Even as we read the Bible in light of tradition, United Methodists also read Scripture within their own particular cultural and experiential contexts. When a United Methodist from the Congo reads that the marginalized Old Testament prophet Elijah was confronted by the priests of foreign gods, she may understand anew the challenges she faces from animist teachings in her own village. Inevitably, her response to the Scripture will be different from the response to that same biblical text by a United Methodist in France or Oregon who is experiencing different faith challenges. Each one of us must determine in our own setting and context how to follow Jesus faithfully. United Methodists cherish the different perspectives each person brings to our interpretation of the Bible.

Finally, as we read the Bible through the lenses of Christian tradition and human experience, we discover how God's Word encourages us to use our God-given reason. God gave us minds, and we are expected to use them. Wesley had great confidence in common sense. United Methodist Christians enter into a profound dialogue with Scripture through tradition, experience, and reason to discern God's call to us.

How do Scripture, tradition, experience, and reason help you sort through issues of Christian faith?

Interpreting the Bible

The quadrilateral helps us interpret the Bible appropriately. Too often, a few specific words of the Bible may be used in ways that ultimately are not in alignment with the whole of Scripture and especially the teachings of Jesus. Even at Jesus's temptation in the wilderness, the devil quoted Scripture out of context, hoping that Jesus would lose his focus on God (Matthew 4:1-10).

Sally knows firsthand the importance of interpreting Scripture through the lens of tradition, experience, and reason. Sally was an active member of her home Baptist church. Following the examples of her parents and grandmothers, she was at church for Sunday school, worship services on Sunday morning, Sunday night, and Wednesday night, choir practice, youth group, and Friday morning prayer breakfast.

She was serious about reading the Bible, alone in her devotional time and with others at Sunday school and worship. At a Wednesday night worship service during high school, she heard a missionary share his experiences teaching and working with people in a far-off country. While the missionary reflected on the word of the prophet Isaiah, "Then I heard the LORD's voice saying, 'Whom should I send, and who will go for us? I said, 'I'm

19

here, send me'" (Isaiah 6:8), Sally heard God's voice prompting her to go into ministry.

Sally mulled over that Scripture for years. She majored in religion in college, attended divinity school, and wondered about ordination. Her father, a Baptist deacon, had always been taught that women could not be pastors. As Scripture says, "Like in all the churches of God's people, the women should be quiet during the meeting. They are not allowed to talk. Instead, they need to get under control, just as the Law says. If they want to learn something, they should ask their husbands at home. It is disgraceful for a woman to talk during the meeting" (1 Corinthians 14:33b-35).

But Sally's dad saw things differently once she told him that God was calling her to be a pastor. He talked about all the faithful women in his life. Just as God had used these women, God could use her. The pastor in her home congregation told her father that he planned to ask Sally to preach in worship one Sunday. Before she could preach, however, the lay leadership committee met and took back the invitation. No woman, not even one who had grown up in that congregation, could be permitted to preach.

How did the quadrilateral help Sally and her father make sense of this conflict? Throughout the Bible, women, such as Miriam, Deborah, and Mary Magdalene were called to share God's good news and lead God's people. Women were active in the first days of the church, as Peter, quoting the Old Testament prophet Joel, preached on the day of Pentecost: *"In the last days, God says, I will pour out my Spirit on all people. Your sons and daughters will prophesy"* (Acts 2:17). Women were leaders in the early church, including Phoebe (Romans 16:1), Junia (Romans 16:7), Tabitha (Acts 9:36-43), and Lydia (Acts 16:14). Sally is a United Methodist pastor because our denomination recognized and affirmed her call by God. One verse of Scripture in one place does not negate a broader understanding of the biblical witness.

Throughout the history of the church, Christians have highlighted certain texts as crucial for their understanding of the Christian faith and practice, even as they downplayed or ignored other texts. Most Christians do not observe the dietary rules in Leviticus about eating pork and shellfish. We no longer send people with skin disease out of the community. Not many Christians faithfully give God 10 percent of their income. Some biblical rules are treated as no longer essential.

It is good that United Methodists have let go of stoning as a form of capital punishment for sins of idolatry, murder, and adultery. Slavery, while at times taken for granted in the Bible, is no longer supported by our denomination. Unfortunately, for almost one hundred years the former Methodist Episcopal Church literally divided over the practice of slavery, and both sides used the Bible to condemn or condone slavery and one another. Thankfully, with tradition, experience, and reason we no longer tolerate the practice of slavery. With the quadrilateral, United Methodists are guided to be faithful disciples of Jesus Christ.

Can you think of a current social issue that the quadrilateral helps give guidance?

The Biblical Message of Grace

For United Methodists, as Andy's father discovered through his study of the history of Methodist theology, the primary message of the Bible is God's grace. Grace is emphasized throughout the Bible from the story of Creation to the description of the end of history. God's grace is most evident in Jesus's life, death, and resurrection. As the Gospel writer John proclaimed, the Word of God "became flesh and made his home among us," and "from his fullness we have all received grace upon grace" (John 1:14, 16). God's grace embodied in Jesus brings us into a right relationship with God and enables us to grow in our love for God and others.

God's grace is present everywhere and always available to us. As Wesley wrote, "The grace or love of God, whence cometh our salvation, is free in all, and free for all."[12] Through grace, God stirs up in us a desire to seek God, summons us to repentance, pardons us, claims us as new people, gives us hope of life abundant and eternal, and seeks to perfect our love of God. Through grace, we are empowered to be more and more like Christ and go out to serve the world. We will return to this theme of grace in chapter 4 about United Methodist beliefs.

John Newton, who wrote the hymn "Amazing Grace," was a friend of Wesley and they corresponded with one another. Newton's own words on his tombstone sum up his life: "John Newton, clerk, once an infidel and libertine, a servant of slaves in Africa, was, by the rich mercy of our Lord and Saviour Jesus Christ preserved, restored, pardoned and appointed to preach the faith he had long labored to destroy" (The Church of Saints Peter and Paul, Olney, England). God's grace shaped the lives of Wesley, Newton, and the millions of people who followed after them.

As Kelia read and listened to Scripture in one of Andy's congregations, grace changed her life. Kelia did not grow up in a church, and most of her contacts with Christians had been negative. Years before, when she and her fiancé sought to be married, pastors turned them away because this was not for them a first marriage. But one Christmas morning, Kelia came to an informal worship service and heard the story of the birth of Jesus. Over the next few years, she occasionally returned to worship, sat on the back row, and listened to Bible stories she had never heard before. Kelia then took a huge risk and signed up for a year-long Bible study, using a United Methodist program called *Disciple*. The group gathered weekly to discuss the Bible and its impact on their lives. During those weeks of study, discussion, and reflection, Kelia became a disciple of Christ. When the class ended, Kelia asked to be baptized and join the church. Through the Bible and among other United Methodists, Kelia experienced God's grace.

How have you experienced grace?

Become a Bible Moth

Today in United Methodist congregations and settings all around the world, persons gather around the Bible. In our private devotions, we read Scripture and reflect on its meaning in our daily lives. We gather in classrooms and living rooms to study the Word using United Methodist resources and other studies. At worship, we hear the Bible read and proclaimed. Through hymns and songs, we sing scriptural prayers and teach our children to sing, "Jesus loves me! This I know, for the Bible tells me so."[13] We pray the Lord's Prayer. And so it is that we United Methodist Christians discover through the Bible a new and renewed relationship with God and one another.

In Wesley's "Preface to *Explanatory Notes upon the Old Testament*," he outlined how Methodists should read the Bible.[14] We paraphrase Wesley's suggestions:

1. Set apart a little time every morning and evening.
2. Read a chapter out of the Old Testament and one out of the New Testament; or simply read a single chapter or part of one chapter.
3. Read this Scripture with a desire to discern God's will and to do God's will.
4. Before and after you read, pray that what you read may be written on your heart.

5. While you read, frequently pause to examine yourself, both with regard to your heart and life. And whatever you discern, put that insight to use immediately.

How do we live as United Methodist Christians? Follow the example of those Bible Moths in Oxford. Pick up a Bible, read it, listen to it, and study it with other Christians. And when you hear God's Word, respond. Then we will be like John Wesley and the others in our great line of splendor who became the people of the Bible.

Hymn Stanzas

Come, divine Interpreter,
    bring me eyes thy book to read,
ears the mystic words to hear,
    words which did from thee proceed,
words that endless bliss impart,
    kept in an obedient heart.

All who read, or hear, are blessed,
    if your plain commands we do;
of thy kingdom here possessed,
    thee we shall in glory view
when thou comest on earth to abide,
    reign triumphant at thy side.

—Charles Wesley (*The United Methodist Hymnal,* 594)

Notes

1. *The United Methodist Book of Discipline,* "Our Doctrinal Heritage" ¶ 102; "The Articles of Religion of The Methodist Church" and "The Confession of Faith of The Evangelical United Brethren Church" ¶ 104; and "Scripture" in "Our Theological Task" ¶ 105.
2. John Wesley, *The Works of John Wesley: Vol. 9, The Methodist Societies: History, Nature, Design* (Abingdon: Nashville (1989), "The Character of a Methodist" (1743), pp. 31-46.

3. Wesley, *Works: Vol. 1, Sermons 1*, p. 70.

4. *Works: Vol. 2*, "The Scripture Way of Salvation" Sermon 43 (1769), pp. 153-169.

5. *Discipline*, ¶ 104, p. 66.

6. *Ibid.*, ¶ 105, p. 83.

7. Andy was a reader consultant in the creation of the Common English Bible.

8. Andy chaired the international, ecumenical committee that created the 1992 Revised Common Lectionary.

9. *Discipline*, "Our Theological Task," ¶ 105.

10. *Works: Vol. 1, Sermons 1*, "Scriptural Christianity" Sermon # 4 (1744), pp. 159-180.

11. *Discipline*, "Doctrinal Standards," ¶ 103.

12. *Works, Vol. 4, Sermons 3*, Sermon 110, "Free Grace" (1739), pp. 542-563.

13. *The United Methodist Hymnal*, 191.

14. John Wesley's "Preface to *Explanatory Notes upon the Old Testament*," Edinburgh, April 25, 1765; https://www.swartzentrover. com/cotor/E-Books/BookScans/Wesley%20-%20John%20Wesley's%20 Notes%20-%20The%20Old%20Testament.pdf.

2. What Do We Share with Other Christians?

United Methodist Christians are a vital part of Christ's universal Church.[1]

Christ is just like the human body—a body is a unit and has many parts; and all the parts of the body are one body, even though there are many. We were all baptized by one Spirit into one body, whether Jew or Greek, or slave or free, and we all were given one Spirit to drink. Certainly, the body isn't one part but many.

1 CORINTHIANS 12:12-14

The Church Universal

United Methodist Christians, while part of a distinct denomination, belong to the global body of Jesus Christ. The church universal has grown and spread for 2,000 years to become the largest religion on the planet with 2.6 billion believers. United Methodists are "loyal heirs to all that [is] best in the Christian past."[2]

Our ancestors in the faith are the Christians gathered in Jerusalem on the Day of Pentecost, early believers persecuted throughout the Roman Empire, members of ancient councils who crafted our creeds, eastern Orthodox Christians who maintained ancient liturgies, medieval theologians who shaped western Christianity, saints who worked with the poor, European Protestant reformers, British Anglicans, and billions of Chris-

27

tians today in millions of congregations north and south of the equator. Each United Methodist follower of Jesus is one with other United Methodists and also one with followers of Jesus of every age and land.

United Methodists identify with the church universal because of John Wesley's own openness to other Christians. In his sermon "Catholic Spirit," Wesley quoted Jehu, the king of Israel, who invited Jehonadab, a leader from a foreign land, to join him in serving God. "Are you as committed to me as I am to you?" Jehu asked Jehonadab. "Yes, I am," Jehonadab answered. "If so," Jehu said, "then give me your hand" (2 Kings 10:15).[3] Wesley exhibited this same open spirit with other Christians.

As a scholar, Wesley read the writings of many theologians throughout the ages. He appreciated the encouragement of the Moravians during his missionary days in Georgia and traveled to Germany to visit the Moravian leader Count Zinzendorf. Wesley and George Whitefield, another outstanding English preacher, often disagreed on points of theology. Even so, Wesley followed Whitefield's advice to preach outside of church buildings in fields, mines, and even on his father's gravestone.

When the Methodist movement crossed the Atlantic to North America, the Methodists initially kept close ties to the Church of England. Increasingly, Methodists then served alongside German evangelicals and United Brethren pietists. In the early 1800s, Methodists and Presbyterians preached side by side at outdoor revival services on the western frontier of America. In the late nineteenth century, many American denominations worked together to send missionaries, more than half of whom were women, around the world. In 1909, Central Methodist Church in Concord, North Carolina, listed two full-time staff, the male pastor, and Lelia Tuttle, a thirty-one-year-old woman serving in China. Today United Methodists are committed to working with and learning from many different Christian traditions in over 130 countries. We affirm the universal church.

In which religious tradition did you grow up?

A Common History

The United Methodist Church shares a common history with Christian communions around the world. United Methodists recognize our beginnings in the church on the Day of Pentecost. The fire of Pentecost still shines in the official logo of our denomination—the cross and flame. We stand in agreement with the classic, ecumenical affirmations of the church, the Apostles' Creed and the Nicene Creed, both of which are in our *United Methodist Hymnal* (880 and 881). In addition, we include in our hymnal statements of faith by the United Church of Canada, the Korean Methodist Church, and a World Methodist Social Affirmation. While United Methodists are not required to affirm any of these creeds for membership in our denomination, these creeds serve as theological foundations.

Although United Methodists honor the contributions of the Eastern Orthodox churches, we have been shaped primarily by western Christianity. Our teachers include Augustine of northern Africa in the fourth century and Aquinas of Italy in the thirteenth century. We are thankful for Roman Catholic saints such as Benedict who taught us to pray, St. Francis of Assisi who showed us how to live simply, and Mother Teresa of Calcutta who demonstrated selfless service. Our United Methodist family tree includes all these saints and traditions.

United Methodists have a direct kinship with the Church of England, which was formed out of the Roman Catholic Church in the 1530s by King Henry VIII. This new denomination retained elements of its Roman Catholic heritage, while primarily aligning with Protestant reformers. The Anglicans kept a high view of the sacraments of baptism and Holy Communion but recognized only these two sacraments. They read Scripture in English and refused to recognize the authority of the pope in Rome. Like the Roman Catholics, the English observed the Christian Year and daily services of prayer. Like the Protestants, the Church of England welcomed married priests. The Church of England understood itself as a middle way between the Roman Catholic and Protestant traditions.

Throughout his life, Wesley remained a faithful priest within the Church of England. He saw the early Methodists as reformers within the Anglican communion, as a gathering of serious Christians called to be the muscle of a church that had grown spiritually weak. Following the American Revolution, however, Wesley heard the plea of Methodists in North America for their own ordained clergy who could baptize, marry, and share Holy Communion. In response, he sent Coke, Whatcoat, and Vasey to initiate the new denomination. We will discuss what happened next among the Methodists in the following chapter.

What religious traditions have defined your life?

The Trinity

While distinctive in many ways, United Methodists accept most major beliefs of other orthodox Christians. We are Christians first, United Methodists second. As a sign of the essential oneness of the church of Jesus Christ, we accept all persons baptized in other Christian communions as sisters and brothers in Christ.

Central to these common beliefs is our affirmation of the Triune God—Father, Son, and Holy Spirit—by which God has been revealed in three distinct but inseparable persons. When United Methodists baptize, we like other Christians do so in the name of the Holy Trinity. As Wesley wrote, "The knowledge of the Three-in-One God is interwoven with all true Christian faith."[4]

How does one describe the mystery of the Trinity, one God in three persons? Our one God has three expressions who are infinite in power, wisdom, justice, goodness, and love. In the final analysis, however, we cannot contain God within our definitions. When Job challenged God to explain the unjust suffering in Job's life, God spoke to Job asking, "Where were you when I laid the earth's foundation? Tell me if you know" (Job 38:4). When Job heard God's litany of the wonders of creation, Job confessed, "I have indeed spoken about things I didn't understand" (Job 42:3). Like Job, United Methodists admit that God cannot be limited by our understanding yet believe that the Trinity makes clear God's self-revelation to us.

The first person of the Trinity, God the Father and Creator, reminds us that God formed every person in God's own image. Stand outside on a clear, dark night and look up at the stars. Remember being delighted by the splendor of a colorful rainbow. The psalmist said it well: "Heaven is declaring God's glory; the sky is proclaiming his handiwork" (Psalm 19:1). Because of our understanding of God as Creator, United Methodists strongly advocate that all people are our siblings and that we must take care of our natural environment.

The second person of the Trinity, Jesus of Nazareth, makes visible God's love for the world. We believe that Jesus Christ is both fully human and fully divine. Christ's divinity was revealed through his presence at Creation, while Jesus's death on the cross expressed his humanity. Because Jesus was a suffering servant, God has highly exalted him, and one day everyone will confess that "Jesus Christ is Lord" (Philippians 2:6-11). Our United Methodist passion to serve our neighbors arises out of our allegiance to Jesus who washed his disciples' feet.

The four Gospels of the Bible—Matthew, Mark, Luke, and John—give witness to Jesus's life, death, and resurrection. Jesus's teachings often run counter to the teachings of the secular world. Society encourages us to be consumers of the world's goods and seek security in our money, possessions, and social status. In contrast, Jesus says, "All who want to save their lives will lose them. But all who lose their lives because of me and because of the good news will save them" (Mark 8:35). Jesus expects his followers to devote their whole being to loving and serving God and all people. Jesus's resurrection ultimately assures us that following Jesus brings life. Because God raised Jesus from the dead, we believe that we, too, will live forever.

United Methodists also know God through the activity of the third person of the Trinity, the Holy Spirit. In our personal lives and in the life of the church, the Holy Spirit comforts, sustains, and empowers us. The practices of the early followers of Jesus in Jerusalem, after they experienced the Holy Spirit on the Day of Pentecost, reveal the person of the Spirit. The first three thousand Christians "devoted themselves to the apostles' teaching, to the community, to their shared meals, and to their prayers" (Acts 2:42). Everyone was filled with awe, and the apostles accomplished many wonders and miraculous signs. All those believers shared what they had with one another; they sold what they owned and gave freely to those in need. The faith of the Christians was contagious, for "the Lord added daily to the community those who were being saved" (Acts 2:47). Similarly, United Methodists filled with the Holy Spirit read the Bible, worship together, share Holy Communion, pray, witness miracles, give generously, and share the good news with others.

How does the Trinity help you speak about God?

Other Basic Christian Affirmations

Along with the Trinity, United Methodists share additional theological beliefs with other Christians. We believe in salvation in and through Jesus Christ. Jesus is the living embodiment of God's grace. We believe that we can experience God's redemptive love in our personal lives and in the church with other believers. Grace is not theoretical but real. We believe in the authority of Scripture and see the church always in need of reform and renewal. All of these beliefs are shared broadly throughout the church universal.

Protestant Christians, including United Methodists, have two additional core beliefs: an emphasis on salvation by grace through faith and the priesthood of all believers. The Protestant movement began in the 1500s as a reaction against some core Roman Catholic beliefs such as the number of sacraments, the role of priests, and the authority of the pope.

Our emphasis on salvation by grace through faith is based on Scripture, in particular the words of the apostle Paul: "You are saved by God's grace because of your faith. This salvation is God's gift. It's not something you possessed. It's not something you did that you can be proud of" (Ephesians 2:8-9).[5] Like other Protestant Christians, we have an absolute confidence in that we are brought into a right relationship with God not by any act or good work we do but by the free, undeserved love of God for us through Jesus Christ.

Another key Protestant belief is that all Christians are commissioned through baptism to be ministers of the gospel of Jesus Christ. God calls Christians to "minister wherever Christ would have them serve and witness in deeds and words that heal and free."[6] All Christians, not only ordained clergy, serve God and other people by their prayers, presence, gifts, service, and witness.

Because we believe in the priesthood of all believers, many units of The United Methodist Church, including General Conferences, are led by equal numbers of laity and clergy. In local churches, a lay-led church council guides the ministries and missions of a whole congregation.

Are you comfortable with these core Christian beliefs?

What's Similar? What's Different?

Having identified what we share in common with other Christians, how is The United Methodist Church like and unlike other major denominations? Ann is part of an ecumenical cohort of pastors who regularly discuss their religious similarities and differences. The United Methodist Church has formal communal agreements with the Moravian, Episcopalian, and Lutheran denominations, and has ongoing dialogue with other communions. While we always remember that we are more alike than different, United Methodists do have theological and organizational distinctions with other churches. In broad strokes, how do we compare and contrast with other Christian denominations?

The Roman Catholic Church, the largest denomination in the

world, is like us by having strong bishops and a global perspective. Roman Catholics differ from United Methodists in that they have seven sacraments, prescribed rituals, celibate male priests, and the pope is the final authority.

Like the Eastern Orthodox churches, including the Greek, Antiochian, and Coptic, United Methodists appreciate the worship practices of the early church. Our worship, on the other hand, has changed in a variety of styles through the ages and we worship in local languages. Ann and Andy attended an hours-long midnight Easter Vigil at the Greek Orthodox Cathedral in Nashville, Tennessee; Sally and Andy attended a three-hour Ascension of the Lord service in a Greek Orthodox Cathedral off the coast of Greece. We celebrate that United Methodists have ongoing theological dialogue and mission activities with both the Roman Catholic and Eastern Orthodox traditions.

United Methodists more clearly belong to the Protestant family of communions. A number of Protestant denominations, including the Baptist, Episcopalian, Lutheran, Pentecostal, and Presbyterian, share our belief in the two sacraments of baptism and Holy Communion, salvation by grace through faith, the priesthood of all believers, and Scripture as our final authority. Yet there are differences.

Baptists, out of a European reform movement, emphasize adult baptism by immersion and the full independence of local congregations. Some Baptists are also biblical fundamentalists and do not ordain women. In The United Methodist Church, we are firmly connected with other United Methodists locally and globally. In our United Methodist denomination, we honor different modes of baptism for persons of all ages, interpret Scripture in light of tradition, experience, and reason, ordain women, and have clergy appointed by bishops. While Andy and Sally's daughters were baptized with the sprinkling of water as infants, Sally celebrated her baptism by immersion at age nine in a Baptist congregation.

Episcopal congregations, out of the Church of England's Anglican faith, have a strong loyalty to their *Book of Common Prayer*. In addition, Episcopal congregations hire their own pastors. We United Methodists use both our *United Methodist Book of Worship* as well as many other resources for worship. Our pastors are appointed by bishops. Andy is grateful that he once had the opportunity to preach at the Church of England's Westminster Abbey in London.

Lutherans, who follow the traditions of the German Reformer Martin Luther, have an absolute focus on salvation by faith. While believing in salvation by faith, United Methodists also believe that good works are a necessary part of salvation. Unlike Lutheran bishops, United Methodist bishops are responsible for pastoral appointments. Wesley's Aldersgate experience took place while hearing someone read Martin Luther's preface to Paul's Letter to the Romans.

Pentecostals, who honor Wesley as one of their spiritual ancestors, share United Methodism's enthusiasm for the work of the Holy Spirit, but unlike United Methodists, Pentecostals include worship with speaking in tongues. While some of our worship is enthusiastic, speaking in tongues does not characterize our style.

Finally, Presbyterians, who claim John Calvin of Geneva as their founder, emphasize God's sovereign and predestined plan for each person. Implications of this emphasis include unconditional election and limited atonement. United Methodists believe that all persons have free will to choose to be and remain in communion with God. Sally's brother-in-law and niece are both wonderful Presbyterian pastors.

In summary, in spite of differences, United Methodists celebrate our connections with these differing Protestant groups and are often in ministry alongside them. Increasingly, people from a variety of Christian traditions are found in all our congregations. Less than half of all the people who belong to The United Methodist Church were raised in this denomination. Every year we receive many persons into membership by transfer from other denominations. We are a theologically diverse denomination.

Out of which theological tradition did you come? What is similar to the United Methodist beliefs? What's different?

Bonds with Other Communions

The United Methodist Church is not the only denomination that had its beginnings in Wesley's revival. While theological disagreements and social realities have divided various Wesleyan groups over the years, United Methodists are grateful for the connections that remain. Thus, our denomination has continuing relationships with other autonomous and affiliated Methodist conferences with whom we are bound historically, such as The Evangelical Methodist Church of Costa Rica. Andy's congregation helped establish a library in the Costa Rican seminary.

In the United States, the Pan-Methodist Alliance was formed to build bridges between different Methodist denominations. Over the years, leaders of The United Methodist Church and five historically African American denominations, including the African Methodist Episcopal Church and the African Methodist Episcopal Zion Church, regularly meet. The focus of the gatherings is encouragement and appreciation. Sally and Andy have taught at a local A.M.E Zion seminary, where Ann also took classes.

On a global level, the World Methodist Council, formally organized in 1951, has been an association of denominations that claim John Wesley as their spiritual forefather. As Wesley wrote, "I look upon the whole world as my parish."[7] This organization includes eighty member denominations from 132 countries and represents over eighty million people. Methodism at this global level is the third largest Protestant theological tradition.

The World Methodist Council includes The United Methodist Church, the Wesleyan Church, the United Church of Canada, the Uniting Church of Australia, the Salvation Army, the Church of the Nazarene, and distinct Methodist denominations across the world. This umbrella group coordinates missions, resources, and training for Wesleyans across the globe. On behalf of the World Methodist Council, Andy once traveled to Singapore to lead a global gathering of Wesleyan worship professionals who shared with one another current hymnals and books of worship all based on Wesleyan theology. The independent Singapore Methodist Church and Malaysian Methodist Church have adopted our *United Methodist Hymnal* as their own for their English-speaking congregations.

Within the wider Christian communion in the United States, The National Council of the Churches of Christ in the USA and the Churches Uniting in Christ are coalitions of many different Christian faith groups. The United Methodist Church contributes to these ministries and receives in return resources such as the International Sunday School Lesson Series. At the same time that national associations of churches were being formed, The World Council of Churches, initially led by Methodists, also began. For over one hundred years, the World Council of Churches has been an international Christian ecumenical organization. This fellowship of over 350 denominations in more than 120 countries now includes almost 600 million Christians.

How do you respond to being part of these grand alliances of Christian communions?

Living and Serving Together

Our commitment to working with other Christians reveals itself in many ways. Because we share our hearts, we readily join hands with our sisters and brothers in Christ. The United Methodist Church has always been one of the most open denominations in joining forces with other Christians for the sake of the kingdom of God.

United Methodists have been at the forefront of ecumenical efforts in mission and outreach both locally and globally. We participate in local community Thanksgiving Celebrations and Holy Week services. In the Philippines, Africa, and Europe, many of the seminaries that train clergy are not exclusively United Methodist but open to many denominations for the training of a new generation of leaders. Together with other Christians, we build hospitals, schools, and agricultural cooperatives. Millard Fuller, the founder of the ecumenical housing ministry Habitat for Humanity, honored The United Methodist Church at our 2000 General Conference for being the most supportive global denomination in building homes for the working poor. This model of cooperation is true wherever one finds United Methodists.

Cooperative Christian Ministry in Cabarrus County, North Carolina, had its formational meeting at Central United Methodist Church. This ministry linked area congregations in service to persons seeking housing and food in the county. For that reason, Roman Catholics, Presbyterians, Lutherans, United Church of Christ members, and members from a dozen other denominations gathered in Central's fellowship hall to plan their cooperative service ministry. Wherever one finds United Methodist congregations you will find similar organizations.

What are the ways your local congregation works with other Christians in your community?

One Body of Christ

Our United Methodist ethos is characterized by our ties to the universal church of Jesus Christ. We proudly say that we are United Methodist, but never in an exclusive way. The apostle Paul compared the church to a human body, explaining that in the same way that a human body needs eyes, ears, hands, and feet to function well, so, too, does the church universal need all of the differently talented and gifted church members to be healthy and whole (1 Corinthians 12). No one Christian or solitary denomination can be the body of Christ in service to the world. No one Christian denomination has exclusive wisdom on how best to be the church in today's society. Where Christians are joining hearts and hands together, we United Methodists are there.

Hymn Stanzas

All praise to our redeeming Lord,
  who joins us by his grace,
and bids us, each to each restored,
  together seek his face. . . .

E'en now we think and speak the same,
  and, cordially agree,
concentered all, through Jesus' name,
  in perfect harmony.

—Charles Wesley (*United Methodist Hymnal*, 554)

Notes

1. *Discipline*, "Our Doctrinal Heritage" ¶ 102, p. 49.
2. *Discipline*, "Episcopal Greetings," p. v.
3. *Works: Vol. 2, Sermons 2*, Sermon 39 "Catholic Spirit" (1750), pp. 79-96.
4. *Works: Vol. 2*, Sermon 55 "On the Trinity" (1775), pp. 373-386.
5. *Discipline*, ¶¶ 126-137.
6. *Ibid.*, ¶ 128.
7. *Works: Vol. 25, Letters I*, "Letter to John Clayton" (March 28, 1739), pp. 614-617.

3. What Is Our United Methodist Story?

United Methodist Christians have an almost three-hundred-year history, full of faithful people and major events.[1]

So then, with endurance, let's also run the race that is laid out in front of us, since we have such a great cloud of witnesses surrounding us.

HEBREWS 12:1

John Wesley

The history of The United Methodist Church begins with the spiritual journeys of John Wesley and the many women and men who followed after him. They are our great cloud of witnesses.

Over the years, many famous persons have been Methodists: American comedian Will Rogers; transformational baseball player Jackie Robinson; three U.S. Presidents: William McKinley, Rutherford B. Hayes, and George W. Bush; author Harper Lee; Civil Rights leader Joseph Lowry; politicians Hillary Clinton and Nikki Haley; singers Beyoncé Knowles and Toni Braxton; in the 115th Congress of the United States ten Senators and thirty members of the House of Representatives; TV game show hosts Pat Sajak and Vanna White; TV home renovators Ben and Erin Napier; and the first woman elected as president of an African nation and winner of the 2011 Nobel Peace Prize winner from Liberia, Ellen Johnson Sirleaf. We are very proud of the famous and the many more not-so-recognized companions in our family tree.

It all started with John Wesley. His life (1703-1791) spanned most of the eighteenth century. His father Samuel, as his father and grandfather before him, was a priest in the Church of England. Samuel cherished the Anglican traditions and served a small, rural congregation in Epworth in northern England for forty years. Susanna, John's mother, also grew up in a clergy family that valued personal holiness. Susanna guided the spiritual disciplines of her family and her husband's church members. Samuel and Susanna were serious Christians who shared a deep love of God. Susanna, who knew both Latin and Greek, led Bible studies in her kitchen and instilled in John an understanding that women, like men, were gifted for Christian leadership. When John questioned the role of women among the early Methodists, his mother reminded him of her own spiritual leadership in her family and her husband's parish.

Through Susanna's influence, women played a crucial role in the Methodist movement. Barbara Heck started the first Methodist class in New York City. In the nineteenth century, women led in mission outreach around the world, particularly among children, women, and the poor. Acceptance of women clergy did not come immediately. In the Methodist Protestant Church, Helenor M. Darisson was ordained as a deacon in 1866, and Anna Howard Shaw was ordained as an elder in 1880. Even so, legislation enacting the full ordination of women in The Methodist Church in 1956 and the election of Marjorie Matthews in 1980 as the first woman bishop of The United Methodist Church can be traced back to the powerful influence of Susanna. Every year more women become United Methodist clergy. United Women in Faith, our organization for women, connects women through mission outreach, spiritual formation, leadership development, and education to shape local and global communities.

Susanna gave birth to nineteen children, ten of whom survived to adulthood. John was her fifteenth child, while Charles, our great hymn-writer, was her seventeenth child. Susanna insisted that the children attend family devotions at dawn, take seriously their academic studies, and pray the Lord's Prayer as soon as they could speak. Her children learned to read the Bible at age five.

In 1709, when five-year-old John was saved from a fire that destroyed the family's parsonage, Susanna dedicated her son's life to God quoting the Old Testament prophet, "a log snatched from the fire" (Zechariah 3:2). At age eleven, John attended a private boys' school in London, where he excelled academically. John read the Scriptures every day, participated in daily prayer services, and attended worship faithfully.

At age seventeen, John attended Oxford University where he trained for the ministry and was ordained as a priest. For two years, John served as his father's associate pastor at Epworth. But at age twenty-two, John decided that he was a better teacher than pastor and moved back to Oxford to teach Greek and rhetoric. Although he was small in size—only five-feet-three-inches tall and weighing 128 pounds throughout his life—John became a powerful force in the church.

How does John Wesley's childhood and early life compare or contrast to your life?

The Beginning of the Methodist Movement

In 1729, Charles, John's brother and entering student at Oxford, invited his twenty-six-year-old brother to lead a Bible study with three members, named the Holy Club. At a time when few people at Oxford took Christianity seriously, the young men read Scripture daily, prayed often, fasted twice a week, visited the local prison, lived modestly, received Holy Communion weekly, and gave money to the poor. Because of the students' methodical Christian practices, other students in Oxford labeled them "Methodists."

Their disciplined Christianity stood in sharp contrast to the English culture of the eighteenth century. The established religious system of small chapels in rural villages, with pastors who lived off endowments, was failing because of several contributing factors. In the Age of Enlightenment, reason not faith was the source of knowledge. The Industrial Revolution transformed English society from a farming culture with extended families to urban, industrialized centers built around mines and factories. Working conditions were harsh, and even young children were forced to work long hours. Distilled alcohol was used widely to blunt the pain of urban life, while the lack of public sanitation led to plagues and smallpox. Tragically, the slave trade supported the country's export economy. And the vast gulf between the rich and the poor extended to religion, where many clergy and wealthy laity worshipped with their eyes closed to the social crises around them.

In 1735, John and Charles both enlisted as missionaries to the new English penal colony in Savannah, Georgia. The brothers shared traditional Anglican practices with the colonists, many of whom had never been in worship, and with the Native Americans, an occupied people. On Sundays, John required everyone to attend worship three times, with the first service beginning at 5:00 a.m. The brothers were spectacularly unsuccessful in their efforts and quickly returned to England, both unsure of their faith.

What is the relationship between your congregation and the people living near your church?

Wesley's Aldersgate Experience

Back in England, John despaired of his failures. He still read the Bible two hours a day, received Holy Communion weekly, fasted twice a week, and taught the Bible. Even so, John doubted his own faith. While in Georgia and upon his return to England, a sect of pious German Moravians urged him to find a personal relationship with God. At age thirty-five in London, just four days after his brother Charles's own religious experience, John had a transformational moment. John described his experience in 1738 this way:

> In the evening I went very unwillingly to a society in Aldersgate Street, where one was reading Luther's preface to the Epistle to the Romans. About a quarter before nine, while the leader was describing the change which God works in the heart through faith in Christ, I felt my heart strangely warmed. I felt I did trust in Christ alone for salvation; and an assurance was given me that He had taken away **my** sins, even **mine**, and saved **me** from the law of sin and death.[2]

Have you had a warm-heart experience?

The First Expansion

For the next fifty-three years, John shared his passionate faith. His heart was on fire with the love of God, and that flame caught people's attention. John spoke at Oxford chapels and in rural congregations and family homes. The year following his Aldersgate experience, John began to preach outdoors to miners and factory workers. John proclaimed the gospel in a closed arms factory, collapsed tin mines, and even on top of his father's tomb. His favorite time of day to preach was 5:00 a.m., before laborers began their workday.

Thousands came to hear Wesley preach, and the results were immediate. His message connected especially with the poor, illiterate, and forgotten underclass. Some people responded to John's preaching with outbursts of prayer and crying. His written sermons were tight theological treatises and bear little relationship to the lively sermons he delivered orally. With tens of thousands of followers, the revival became the major religious movement of eighteenth-century England.

Many leaders within the established church felt threatened by the Wesleyan revival. Preaching outdoors, dynamic hymn-singing, celebrating Holy Communion among the masses, and challenging the reigning religious ethos created great controversy. Many pastors refused to let John preach in their churches, and persons interrupted his preaching with shouting and stone throwing. Yet the more John was opposed, the more this God-movement grew.

United Methodist Christians today follow Wesley's evangelistic fervor. At our best, we share the gospel with everyone, including persons and communities often overlooked. We celebrate when we begin a new Hispanic ministry in a rural county, a biker church in a mountain community, a Bible study at a prison, an inner-city congregation for people facing homelessness, or a new gathering for Bible study and conversation in a coffee shop. When we reach out to others through sharing the gospel in word and deed, we are following in the footsteps of the first Methodists.

Singing became a key characteristic of the Methodist revival. John's brother Charles was a brilliant and prolific poet, writing almost 6,500 religious poems, which he often set to popular and easily sung music. Many Christians learned the Christian faith by singing Charles's hymns. John wrote in the preface in one of his hymnals, "Sing lustily and with a good courage."[3]

When the Methodists in Concord, North Carolina, established a new congregation in 1837 for Whites and Blacks, the town leaders refused to allow the Methodist sanctuary to be built within the city limits because "the Methodists sang too loud." Later, Fanny Crosby, a blind Methodist musician, wrote gospel hymns like "Blessed Assurance." Andy's mother claimed to know more theology through Wesley's hymns than through the preaching of her husband.

Lively singing still characterizes our worship, and *The United Methodist Hymnal* is second only to the Bible in books purchased by local congregations. As storyteller Garrison Keillor wrote, "We make fun of Methodists for their blandness, their excessive calm, their fear of giving offense, their lack of speed, and also for their secret fondness for macaroni and cheese. But nobody sings like them."[4]

Wesley was a brilliant organizer. Building on his earlier experiences in Oxford, John urged people wanting to grow in their faith to join a small group for a weekly meeting for spiritual development. The Methodists established thousands of classes around England, Wales, Ireland, and in the American colonies. Lay preachers watched over the groups and often rotated among the classes in hundreds of cities, towns, and villages. Sunday school classes, Bible studies, and other small groups for Christian formation are heirs of this tradition.

Wesley believed that true commitment to Jesus included commitment to serving others. He established an orphanage, a free medical dispensary, a credit union with micro-loans, food pantries, and clothes closets. Methodists discovered their own leadership skills and became community leaders. They became the foundation of a new middle class in England and later in the United States.

During his lifetime, Wesley traveled 250,000 miles on horseback and preached over 40,000 sermons. He lived on a salary of a public-school teacher and gave away the income he earned as an author. When Wesley died at age eighty-seven, he left behind over 500 preachers, almost 80,000 Methodists in England, 57,000 Methodists in the United States, and clusters of Methodists in a dozen other countries. By the end of his life, Methodism had become a respected and honored community of faith. A statue of Wesley was set at St. Paul's Church of England cathedral in London. As he said on his deathbed, surrounded by friends, "The best of all is, that God is with us."[5]

What does John Wesley mean to United Methodists today? Although we have spent pages describing Wesley, United Methodist Christians are not fixated on this man. He both struggled with his faith and had exceptionally high expectations of himself and his friends. We do not try to imitate Wesley the man but strive for his commitment to following Jesus. United Methodists are not obsessed with our past but instead keep looking for new ways to offer Christ to the world.

What aspect of the early Methodist movement challenges you?

The Movement Spreads to America

The Methodist renewal movement spread to the American colonies. As English Methodists immigrated to the new world, laywomen and laymen established Methodist classes along the eastern seaboard. In 1769, John sent a few lay preachers to strengthen the Methodist societies. The Methodists gathered in homes and small buildings for Bible study, prayer, singing, and service, even as they continued to be baptized and served Holy Communion by priests of the Church of England.

When the American colonies declared their independence from England in 1776, religious institutions in the colonies were scattered, and less than 10 percent of the people belonged to a congregation. The Church of England withdrew its priests from America, leaving the Methodists with no access to the sacraments and services of the church. In 1784, Wesley sent three priests to ordain thirteen clergy, elect two bishops (Thomas Coke and Francis Asbury), and begin a new denomination. The first ever official Methodist denomination was born: The Methodist Episcopal Church.

Episcopal, another word for bishop, simply indicates that the Methodists in America were led by bishops. Each year the bishops gathered the Methodist preachers and together they wrote rules for their work and published hymnals and other resources. The United Methodist Publishing House is the oldest church-owned publishing house in the world. The Methodists in North America now charted their own course.

Francis Asbury (1745-1816) fundamentally shaped the Methodist movement in North America. Born in England, Asbury as a youth joined the Wesleyan revival and became a traveling preacher. In 1771, the twenty-six-year-old Asbury traveled to North America to preach and organize. Asbury never went back to England. During the American Revolution, when most clergy withdrew from the public eye, Asbury remained active in ministry and the Methodists grew to 15,000 members. In 1784, at this first Methodist Conference in Baltimore, Asbury was elected by his peers as a bishop. Asbury never married; instead, the new denomination was his passion. By 1800, the denomination had multiplied to 65,000 members.

Over his ministry of forty-five years, Asbury traveled throughout the eastern states, covering 130,000 miles on horseback, ordaining 4,000 clergy, and preaching more than 16,000 sermons. Asbury's emphases on disciplined piety, small group ministry, evangelism, traveling preachers, and the strong role of the bishop profoundly shaped our United Methodist tradition.

Asbury, committed to our unique practice of itinerancy, sent passionate preachers where they were needed, without regard to location, salary, or family. In the early days of Methodism, the male circuit riders served large geographical regions by horseback for six months at a time. All of North Carolina was served by three circuit riders. After the American Civil War, when clergy began to marry and become more educated, pastors would locate to one parish for one year and then move to a new community. Over time, the length of appointments increased, but still today every United Methodist pastor serves in an appointment made or remade by a bishop each year.

Important traces of the early tradition of circuit riders remain today. Pastors belong to an annual conference, not a local church, and serve not only a local congregation, but also the wider community. Bishops make assignments in the best interest of the whole denomination. Traveling preachers pledge to go where the bishop sends them and serve the world as their parish.

What can we learn from the first Methodists in America?

Other Founding Traditions

As the same time that The Methodist Episcopal Church was established, two other denominations were forming in the United States. Philip Otterbein, a German Reformed pastor, and Martin Boehm, a Mennonite preacher who had read Wesley's sermons, both preached an evangelistic message with an emphasis on personal holiness. At the Methodists' organizing conference in 1784, Otterbein participated in the ordination of Asbury. In 1800, Otterbein and Boehm founded the Church of the United Brethren in Christ, which primarily evangelized German immigrants in the middle-Atlantic states.

Meanwhile, Jacob Albright, a Lutheran farmer who had listened to Methodist preachers and participated in Methodist classes, created the Evangelical Association in 1803, which later joined with the United Brethren and became The Evangelical United Brethren Church. After many twists and turns, all of these denominations joined together in 1968 to create The United Methodist Church.

Can you list the denominations that shaped your family?

The Growth of Methodism

The first decades of the nineteenth century saw dramatic growth in the Methodist movement. As the nation grew, the Methodists sent out more circuit riders to the frontier settlers. Instead of waiting for people to establish a congregation and then call a preacher, young men rode from settlement to solitary house to town to preach, teach, baptize, celebrate Holy Communion, and organize the people in small groups. Most of these preachers owned only the horse they rode, the clothes on their backs, and the books in their bags. Because of the harsh lifestyle, many of these young pastors lasted only a few years in ministry. Thanks to these traveling preachers, one-half of all members of all churches in the United States in 1850 were Methodist.

The Methodists' missionary zeal was extended to countries around the world. By 1833, the first Methodist congregation was formed in Liberia, West Africa; in 1858, Francis Burns became the first African American bishop and served the Liberia area. Subsequently, preachers were sent and congregations formed in China (1847), Germany (1849), and India (1876). Methodists could soon be found in Australia, Norway, Haiti, South Africa, and Tonga.

When the Methodists in North America saw the needs of African Americans and Native Americans, they initiated new ministries. In 1838, when the Cherokee Indians were forced to leave the North Carolina mountains to move to Oklahoma on the Trail of Tears, two Methodist pastors accompanied them. Today, United Methodists remain a strong presence in Native American communities in Oklahoma. At the beginning of the twentieth century, the Methodists in the United States began churches in Korea, and today those congregations are starting new churches throughout Asia. United Methodists now have congregations in over 45 countries and are in mission in over 130 nations.

What can we learn from this missionary zeal?

Division

While the Methodist movement grew greatly in the early 1800s, these years also mark the most difficult chapters in our history. In our first one hundred years, there were nine major divisions around race and the authority of bishops and clergy. At the originating Christmas Conference of 1784, two African American preachers—Richard Allen and "Black Harry" Hosier—were present and active. In response to racism within the church, Allen left the denomination in 1816 and organized The African Methodist Episcopal Church. In 1821, another group of African Americans formed The African Methodist Episcopal Zion Church. In 1830, to establish stronger leadership roles for laity, another group left the denomination and began The Methodist Protestant Church. Thankfully, many African Americans remained with The Methodist Episcopal Church throughout the turmoil. In 1837, when Concord Methodist Episcopal Church began, it included 40 percent African Americans.

The most painful chapter in our denomination occurred before the American Civil War. Despite John Wesley's abhorrence of slavery and efforts to abolish slavery throughout the British Empire, the issue of slavery divided the American denomination. In 1843, the Wesleyan Methodist Church split away when the larger denomination refused to support the abolition of slavery. In 1845, the Methodist Episcopal Church South separated itself from the northern Methodists, and these two groups remained divided until they reunited in 1939.

Our denomination seeks to heal the divisions based on race that remain among us and is committed to being anti-racist and promoting inclusivity and equity. In our history, race has shaped our structures, including the division over slavery in the nineteenth century and the creation of the Central Jurisdiction in the twentieth century. Today, we pursue diverse participation and representation at every level of our church. Women, youth, young adults, physically challenged persons, and persons from every race and ethnic group are chosen as leaders. Recently, The United Methodist Church has had more Native Americans than any other denomination and includes the second largest total of Hispanic persons among all denominations in the United States. We have had African American bishops since 1858. In 1992, Hae Jong Kim became our first Korean bishop; in 2001, Elias Galvan became our first Hispanic bishop; and in 2023, David Wilson became our first Native American bishop. Our official hymnals and books of worship are published also in Spanish and Korean. Around the world, supplemental hymnals are in French, Tongan, Hmong, Native American languages, and German, and include contributions from each culture. When United Methodists gather today, we always ask, "Who is missing from the table?"

What can we learn from these various times of division in our history?

The Church Regains Energy

After the Civil War, the Methodists, in their parallel bodies, grew dramatically. From 1865 to 1913, membership increased 400 percent. During the Gilded Age, United Methodists trained clergy in new theological schools, formed thousands of new congregations, built great sanctuaries from coast to coast, constructed hospitals, and grew missions throughout the United States and around the world. Methodists began Goodwill Industries for the training of the unemployed and established churches in eastern Europe.

The Methodists, Evangelicals, and United Brethren created

over one hundred schools and colleges. A few of the schools include Albright College, Boston University, Duke University, Emory University, Meharry Medical College plus ten other Historically Black Colleges and Universities, Southern Methodist University, Ohio Wesleyan University, Nebraska Methodist College, Alaska Pacific University, and many others in the United States and other countries. Women led missionary efforts both near and far. The churches expanded their ministries among Hispanics, Native Americans, Asian Americans, Pacific Islanders, and African Americans. Methodists addressed social issues such as child labor, workers' unions, and minimum wage laws.

The heirs of the Wesleyan revival also engaged in many theological debates. Some Methodists split to create the Salvation Army, with its focus on social holiness. Holiness and Pentecostal denominations, such as the Assemblies of God, were formed by other Methodists with new emphases on personal holiness and more ecstatic styles of worship. Still other Methodists highlighted the Social Gospel, emphasizing the voice of religion in political affairs, and still others debated the role of Scripture in determining theology.

Methodists led the Prohibition movement against alcohol in the nineteenth and early twentieth centuries. Francis Willard, a leader of the Temperance Movement, when challenged to mind her own business, replied in typical Methodist fashion, "This is God's business." Dr. Thomas B. Welch, a Methodist, created "Methodist Unfermented Communion Wine," which most people now call grape juice. Throughout this period, the Methodists were faithful to their roots and strove always to link vital piety and social witness.

How do United Methodists link vital piety and social witness in your community?

Union Anew

Several of these predecessor denominations successfully united in the twentieth century. In 1939, the Methodists in the north and south, along with The Methodist Protestant Church, joined together to become The Methodist Church. Another union in 1946 among the formerly German denominations created The Evangelical United Brethren, and in 1968, this denomination united with The Methodist Church to form The United Methodist Church. The red in our cross and flame logo has two flames, indicating the union of these two communions. At that time, almost eleven million United Methodists in the United States belonged to one of the largest and wealthiest Protestant bodies in the world.

Since 1968, The United Methodist Church has seen both decline and growth. Our worldwide vision is broader and more inclusive. The role of youth, young adults, laity, women, and many racial and ethnic communities has expanded. In recent years, our membership and influence have grown dramatically throughout the Pacific Islands, Southeast Asia, and Africa. Over half of our thirteen million members now live outside the United States.

Within the United States and Europe, however, our membership and influence have declined. Some observers attribute the losses to our lack of evangelical zeal, while others blame our retreat from controversial social issues. Has our denomination has become more like the established Church of England of the eighteenth century instead of a deeply committed reform movement within the global church? Many United Methodists today are eager to reclaim our emphases on both social and personal holiness and renew the fervor that once characterized the people called Methodists.

Recent Splintering and Fresh Expressions

Most recently, The United Methodist Church has witnessed both splintering and significant new growth. Controversy over the full inclusion of LGBTQIA+ (lesbian, gay, bisexual, transexual, queer, intersexual, asexual, plus others) persons in our denomination has led some United Methodist members and congregations to divide from the denomination. Divisions have also been generated following long disagreements over scriptural interpretation, financial apportionments and expenditures, governance and authority issues, and distribution of power. After much prayer and conversation, about 20 percent of the members and congregations in the United States have withdrawn from our denomination. Some departing congregations have become independent, while others have united with other denominations.

In 2022, the Global Methodist Church was organized. About 3,000+ congregations, most of whom are former United Methodist congregations from the Sunbelt of the United States, have joined this new denomination. A core affirmation of the Global Methodist Church is that LGBTQIA+ persons cannot be ordained as clergy, and congregations shall not allow same-sex weddings.

This splintering has caused much pain for the persons and congregations who are disaffiliating from The United Methodist Church, as well as for those who are choosing to remain. For the remaining United Methodists, however, this time has been ideal for vigorous discussion about the future of The United

Methodist Church and each congregation's and member's role within it.

This very book has been written to help shape the conversation in local churches throughout the connection. Together we can reaffirm our commitment to The United Methodist Church's grace-filled theology and rich diversity of persons and missions. Already, congregations are prayerfully and joyfully renewing their commitments as United Methodists. Central United Methodist Church in Concord, North Carolina, which was organized in 1837 and is now the church home for Sally and Andy, has decided to "affirm to affiliate" and "Be United Methodist."

On the larger level, discussions and debates about a wide range of issues, including who can be ordained or married, will continue within The United Methodist Church. One primary setting for addressing various questions is the General Conference, the only body that sets church law and speaks on behalf of the whole denomination. Hopefully, every discussion and debate will be centered in Christian love. And as United Methodists have continually experienced, God is always doing new things among us, many of which we could never fully predict.

The United Methodist Church remains the strongest mainline denomination in the United States and the largest Methodist denomination in the world. United Methodists have a renewed commitment to serve new people and form new faith communities.

Signs of new growth within the denomination are apparent everywhere. United Methodist communities outside the United States are growing dramatically. With a commitment to the Bible, strong leadership, passionate love of their neighbors, exciting worship, and fidelity to both personal and social holiness, United Methodist congregations in Asia and Africa have continued to multiply. Already the majority of United Methodists live outside the United States.

Within the United States, United Methodists are creating thousands of new faith communities for spiritual persons who are unchurched. Many of these communities are part of an international, ecumenical movement under the broad banner of Fresh Expressions. Like the first Methodists in England and the circuit riders on the American frontier, laity and clergy are reaching out to neighbors, including single moms, refugees, musicians, potters, and paddleboarders. This model of Christian growth includes listening to and loving people, building community, exploring discipleship, and only then developing a congregation. Fresh Expressions, which began in England among Anglicans and Methodists, engenders:

[a] form of church for our changing culture established primarily for the benefit of people who are not yet members of any church. It will come into being through principles of listening, service, incarnational mission and making disciples. It will have the potential to become a mature expression of church shaped by the gospel and the enduring marks of the Church and for its cultural context.[6]

In North Carolina, Fresh Expression communities include a Hispanic community built around soccer and an African American community focused on play, art, storytelling, and Bible study.

As United Methodist pastor Luke Edwards describes Fresh Expressions:

Leaders are trained to reach out to neighbors with shared interests. They meet in community spaces such as a pub, park, or coffee shop. Over drinks or a shared meal, the members listen to the needs of one another, affirm one another, build community, and explore ways of being disciples of Jesus Christ. Rather than waiting for people to come to Sunday morning worship in the sanctuary, these United Methodists are meeting friends and neighbors where they are.[7]

The United Methodist Church continues to be a big-tent denomination, with room enough for people with many differing theological opinions and many ways of worshipping and serving together. While United Methodists are not of one mind on many issues, one of our core values is that in essentials we are unified and in nonessentials flexible. Our United Methodist openness to many perspectives is a major strength.

What do you love about The United Methodist Church today?

Hope and Renewal

Over our history, United Methodists have witnessed much growth and change. Wesley adapted the liturgical practices of the Church of England to reach more people. The circuit riders took the gospel to the western frontier of America. When women were assigned secondary roles within the denomination, they created the largest mission society in North America. After the Iron Curtain fell in Eastern Europe, United Methodists established congregations in Moscow, Warsaw, and Kiev. When we saw a need in Africa for teachers, farmers, clergy, and medical personnel, United Methodists created schools. Our story continues.

Our Council of Bishops have provided an optimistic vision of our denomination:

> All of our members, clergy, local churches, and annual conferences will continue to have a home in the future United Methodist Church, whether they consider themselves liberal, evangelical, progressive, traditionalist, middle of the road, conservative, centrist, or something else.[8]

Our United Methodist story has not yet been fully written. John Wesley could never have imagined that the ministry that began with the Bible Moths of Oxford would touch over eighty million people in many denominations that call him their forefather in the faith. As United Methodist Christians today, our heritage calls us to share the gospel even more widely, invite more people into a relationship with Jesus Christ, challenge more boldly the forces of evil in our world, and let the Holy Spirit burn in us ever more brightly.

Hymn Stanzas

And are we yet alive,
    and see each other's face?
Glory and thanks to Jesus give
    for his almighty grace! . . .

Let us take up the cross
    till we the crown obtain,
and gladly reckon all things loss
    so we may Jesus gain.

—Charles Wesley (*The United Methodist Hymnal*, 553)

Notes

1. *The Book of Discipline* opens with a "Brief History of The United Methodist Church," pp. 11-24. There are many other good histories of this denomination.

2. *Works: Vol. 18, Journal and Diaries*, pp. 249-50.

3. Wesley, "Directions for Singing" (1761), *The United Methodist Hymnal*, p. vii.

4. Garrison Keillor on "Those People called Methodists," https://www.beliefnet.com/columnists/bibleandculture /2007/02/garrison-keillor-on-those-people-called-methodists.html.

5. Wesley, *Letters VIII* (London: Epworth Press, 1931), (March 2, 1791), p. 267.

6. Stephen Croft, editor, *Mission-Shaped Questions: Defining Issues for Today's Church* (New York: Seabury Books, 2010), p. 9.

7. Quotation of Luke Edwards from conversations with Andy Langford, May 2023, based on Edwards's *How to Start a New Kind of Church* (ebook, 2023) and *Becoming Church: A Trail Guide for Starting Fresh Expressions* (2021), available at https://freshexpressions.com.

8. "A Narrative for the Continuing United Methodist Church" (November 2021).

4. What Do United Methodists Believe?

United Methodists have a laser focus on God's grace.[1]

Jesus said, "A certain man had two sons. The younger son said to his father, 'Father, give me my share of the inheritance.' Then the father divided his estate between them. Soon afterward, the younger son gathered everything together and took a trip to a land far away. There, he wasted his wealth through extravagant living. . . .

"When [the son] came to his senses, he said, 'How many of my father's hired hands have more than enough food, but I'm starving to death! I will get up and go to my father, and say to him, "Father, I have sinned against heaven and against you."' . . .

"While [the younger son] was still a long way off, his father saw him and was moved with compassion. His father ran to [his son], hugged him, and kissed him. Then his son said, 'Father, I have sinned against heaven and against you. I no longer deserve to be called your son.' But the father said to his servants, 'Quickly, bring out the best robe and put it on him! Put a ring on his finger and sandals on his feet! Fetch the fattened calf and slaughter it. We must celebrate with feasting because this son of mine was dead and has come back to life! He was lost and is found!' And they began to celebrate."

LUKE 15:11-24

Practical Divinity

John Wesley was not an academic theologian. His theology was not systematic but pragmatic and missional with the goal of assisting people along a path of salvation. Wesley understood himself as a folk theologian, speaking "plain truth for plain people."[2] His vision was "to reform the nation, particularly the Church, and to spread scriptural holiness over the land."[3]

Andy's father described Wesley's theology as "practical divinity." As the core of this practical theology, Wesley understood the Gospel of John 1:16: "grace upon grace." Wesley promoted preaching the gospel, serving the world, and organizing Christians to share that grace. "Theology . . . was to be preached, sung, and lived."[4]

Wesley's definition of Methodists in his pamphlet, "The Character of a Methodist," which we quoted in the first chapter, illustrates this practical theology:[5]

1. The distinguishing marks of Methodists are not their opinions of any sort. . . . But as to all opinions which do not strike at the root of Christianity, we think and let think. . . .

2. We do not place our religion, or any part of it, in being attached to any peculiar mode of speaking. . . .

3. Nor do we desire to be distinguished by actions. . . .

5. "What then is the mark? Who is a Methodist? . . ." I answer: Methodists are they who have "the love of God shed abroad in their hearts. . . . ;" ones who "love the Lord God with all their hearts, and with all their souls, and with all their minds, and with all their strength." . . .

17. These are the marks of a true Methodist. . . . If anyone says, "Why, these are only the common fundamental principles of Christianity!" . . . this is the very truth.

United Methodists today exhibit this same character. In response to God's grace, United Methodists seek to love God completely and share that love with others. In this chapter, we share how God's grace is present in all of creation and has the potential to transform every person into a fully committed disciple of Jesus Christ.

How do you respond to Wesley's definition of "The Character of a Methodist"? What appeals to you? What challenges you?

Emphasis on Grace

Throughout Wesley's practical theology, several themes emerge. None of these perspectives are unique to us, but our emphases upon a few of them are distinctive.[6]

Based on Scripture, the primacy of God's grace stands as our United Methodist core theological affirmation. For United Methodists, grace has been the "pivot point" and "creative center" and "criterion for judging theological value."[7] Throughout the Bible, we see God's grace revealed, especially in the life, death, and resurrection of Jesus Christ. United Methodists describe our experiences of grace as a series of interactions with God, which we call prevenient grace, justifying grace and assurance, and sanctifying grace and perfection.

United Methodists see these moments of grace throughout our lives as we journey toward salvation: God calls us and we listen (prevenient grace); God embraces us and we trust (justifying grace); and God empowers us and we live faithfully (sanctifying grace). United Methodists see these

67

grace-filled moments illustrated in the parable of the wayward son, Wesley's own faith journey, and our own spiritual journeys of salvation.

Where have you experienced grace in your life?

The Journey of Salvation

A fundamental question that every Christian must answer is what does it mean to be saved? For some Christians, salvation depends on receiving the sacraments of the church. For other Christians, salvation comes when one makes a public profession of faith and is baptized by immersion. For still other Christians, the way of salvation involves speaking in tongues. United Methodists believe that all of these experiences of grace are real, yet none of them alone encompasses the whole of God's love for us. We do not save ourselves; God is always the source of grace in many ways and at every moment.

The way of salvation with the varieties of grace as signposts can be described as a journey. This journey covers many roads with numerous twists and turns. Different traveling companions accompany us. This path of salvation has strange bypaths and frequent stops. Throughout this journey, each person has the freedom to stop, go in another direction, or head back from where one came. All of us are on this lifelong journey, but no two people take the same steps in the same manner. And, at every step, God's grace is present.

As Wesley wrote:

What is *salvation*? The salvation which is here spoken of is not what is frequently understood by that word, the going to heaven, eternal happiness. . . . It is not a blessing which lies on the other side death. . . . It is . . . a present thing, a blessing which, through the free mercy of God, ye are now in possession of. . . . Salvation . . . might be extended to the entire work of God, from the first dawning of grace in the soul till it is consummated in glory.[8]

When someone asks, "Are you saved?" how do you respond?

Prevenient Grace

Our salvation journey begins before we are even aware of God. Before we seek God, God is already seeking us. Prevenient grace recognizes that God's love comes before we do anything to deserve God's love. God is always present everywhere and to everyone.

All humans, unfortunately, exhibit a self-centeredness that fundamentally severs our relationship with God; we call this estrangement from God sin. Sin corrupts not only our connection with God, but also with other persons and the whole of creation. Yet, despite our failures, God's prevenient grace gives us the capacity to sense the underlying presence of God. God's love surrounds us and prompts our first response to draw near to God.

We see prevenient grace in Jesus's story about the runaway son. From the moment of the son's birth and long before the son could reciprocate, the father loved his son. The father willingly gave his son freedom to make his own decisions, even when the son demanded his inheritance early. When Wesley questioned his own faith, God continued to work in Wesley's life through his friends, family, and experiences.

For us, even when we are too busy or distracted to hear, God keeps calling us. God may speak to us at the beginning of our salvation journey in an everyday conversation or when our conscience prompts us to act. We may hear God whispering to us while we pray or read the Bible, or when we reflect on a sermon or receive Holy Communion. At significant moments in our lives—when we begin a new job, get married, or have a child—we often sense God's presence with us. When our world seems to be falling apart—a child dies, a relationship ends, or financial security is lost—we may experience God drawing us close.

When United Methodists baptize an infant, before the child is even aware of God, we affirm that God is already claiming the infant as a member of the household of God. At their baptisms as babies, Andy and Ann both believe that their journeys of salvation had begun. Our only response to this quiet, persistent love is to say, "Thank you, God." The way of salvation had begun.

How have you experienced prevenient grace?

Justifying Grace and Assurance

We have all failed and need God's forgiveness. That is our human condition. Hungry and alone, the younger son lamented his ruined life. Unable to make things better on his own, the son began his journey home. When the younger son understood how badly he had failed, he said, "I'm sorry." Wesley had many dark nights of the soul after his failed missionary trip to Georgia. He knew his need for God's forgiveness.

All of us know that we are not the people God created us to be. Along our spiritual journeys, moments arise when God causes us to become discontent with our present lives. Perhaps we question our achievements and values or wonder why we engage in activities that do not bring us fulfillment. Maybe we realize that we are overly concerned with our jobs, possessions, or families. Whenever we confess that our lives are self-centered, whenever we notice how far we have traveled down the wrong path, God's justifying grace opens our eyes. At this stage in our salvation journey, we say to Jesus, "Re-direct me."

Justifying grace may be experienced over a lifetime or in a single dramatic moment, but whenever we turn from sin and toward God, Jesus Christ welcomes us and restores us to God's kingdom. God forgives us, offers us new birth, and calls us children of God. The physical sign of justifying grace is baptism or a reaffirmation of baptismal vows, when a person stands before God and a congregation and says, "I believe." One further expression of justifying grace is the assurance we gain that we are God's children. We have profound trust in God, not based on the strength of our faith, but divinely given confidence that we are in communion with God.

The runaway son experienced God's justifying grace and assurance. When the son was still some distance from home, his father, who had watched constantly for his son's return, saw him and rushed to embrace him. Even as the son begged for forgiveness, the father prepared a welcome home feast. Never again did the son question his father's love. Wesley experienced a moment of justifying grace at the Bible study on Aldersgate Street, and from then on, expressed his assurance of God's love.

Some people speak of this moment of reorientation toward God as conversion. United Methodists speak of conversion less often as one event and more often as a process. Our conversion may be sudden and dramatic or gradual and cumulative. Some people journey toward God from the moment of their baptism as an infant, while other people become Christians through a significant experience as youth or adults. When Sally was nine years old, she walked to the front of her Baptist sanctuary and asked to be baptized. This change in a person's life marks a new beginning, yet it also takes a whole lifetime to unfold.

How have you experienced justifying grace and assurance?

Sanctifying Grace and Perfection

The final stage in our journey with Jesus, sanctifying grace, is God's ongoing work in our lives to make us whole and perfect in our love for God and our neighbor. Sanctification means to be made holy and love God completely.

We can only speculate about sanctifying grace in the life of the younger son. We do not know what happened after the father welcomed him home. Did the son remain faithful, working each day in the fields? Did he repay the money he had squandered? We do not know; but, because of the father's love, we suspect that the son's life changed for the better.

We do know how sanctifying grace affected Wesley after his heart-warming experience at Aldersgate. Wesley never relied on that one experience or said complacently, "I have been saved, and nothing more is expected of me." Instead, Wesley sought continually to become more holy in his personal piety and passion to serve others. While Wesley never claimed to be perfect, or even to have met any perfect person, he strove for perfection, not as a human accomplishment, but as a gracious gift from God.

Similarly, United Methodists do not stop their journey of salvation with any one experience of God's grace. Through Bible study, prayer, and worship we grow closer to God. Through our outreach to people in our local communities and around the world, we grow more loving. Throughout our lives, we must be nurtured by other Christians and empowered by God to become the loving people God created us to be. Sanctification and perfection remind us that the Holy Spirit works within us, seeking to make us whole in love.

The journey of salvation is not complete without all these moments or stages of God's grace. Having heard God's call and answered, having felt God's judgment and repented, and having been embraced by God and responded in trust, we are undergirded by God's strength and encouraged to keep growing toward complete love. Frances, a ninety-five-year-old in Ann's congregation still reads the Bible daily, saying: "God's not done with me yet!" Jesus invites us to be lifelong followers, saying to God over and over again: "Re-form me. Re-shape me. Make me like you."

How are you still trying to grow as a follower of Jesus Christ?

The Variety of Salvation Journeys

This lifelong journey with Jesus through all these grace-filled moments is what United Methodists mean by salvation. We know Jesus in our hearts and heads, and we serve Jesus with our lips, hands, and feet. Jesus loves us before we love him, and then offers us forgiveness, assurance, and a holy life. All that Jesus requires of us is a willingness to listen, to kneel, to trust, and to serve.

No two journeys with Jesus are the same. Our turning to God may be dramatic or quiet, emotional or intellectual, instantaneous or gradual, or a combination of all the above. What is common in all these journeys, however, is that each life-changing experience is initiated by God, who engages each of us as individuals and allows for our own individual, freely given responses. Life-changing moments happen throughout our lives, because at every moment we may hear the voice of God and decide once again to follow Jesus.

How do you describe your journey with Jesus?

Emphasis on Telling the Good News

Because we are recipients of God's grace and are experiencing salvation, United Methodist Christians are an evangelistic people. We eagerly invite other people to share the spiritual journey with us. Once we have experienced God's grace, we joyfully proclaim the good news of God's love with others.

Wesley was passionate about sharing his experience of God's prevenient, justifying, and sanctifying grace. The Methodists who traveled to the United States, the circuit riders who rode on the frontier, and the missionaries who traveled to Africa, eastern Europe, and Asia were all committed to tell others about God's grace.

Reflecting our understanding of the inclusivity of grace, our *Discipline* declares that everyone can be part of The United Methodist Church:

All persons without regard to race, color, national origin, status, or economic condition, shall be eligible to attend its worship services, participate in its programs, receive the sacraments, upon baptism be admitted as baptized members, and upon taking vows declaring the Christian faith, become professing members in any local church.[9]

Today, United Methodists in Vienna, Austria, share the message of God's love with immigrants from Africa and Asia, while missionaries from Korea and Africa share their faith with citizens of the United States. We celebrate that The United Methodist Church has congregations in Vietnam, Ukraine, and Angola. All of these new faith communities have arisen because of our ongoing passion to invite others to experience the fullness of God's grace. In Anchorage, Alaska, there are two new United Methodist congregations: Every Nation UMC for native peoples and Ola Toe Fuataina (New Beginnings) UMC for Samoan people.

Have you ever shared your faith journey with someone else?

Think and Let Think

In all theological matters, United Methodists are open to differences in perspectives and opinions. Over the generations, Methodist theologians have been part of various theological camps. While such openness can be frustrating to people who want quick, easy, and final answers, we keep probing for new insights from God. Not one of us has a monopoly on the truth or fully understands the mind of God.

John Wesley's favorite dictum was, "As to all opinions which do not strike at the root of Christianity, we think and let think."[10] In United Methodist Sunday school classes, at gatherings of laity or clergy, and in many other settings, one can always expect a multitude of passionate opinions. Whether the topic is a Christian response to global warming, or human sexuality, or economic systems, we may choose to disagree. In 1996, when Democrat Bill Clinton and Republican Bob Dole ran against one another to be president of the United States, they had both recently attended Foundry United Methodist Church in Washington, D.C. Whenever new and longtime United Methodists discuss contemporary topics or when a United Methodist from the Republic of Zambia discusses an issue with a United Methodist from Norway, everyone listens, learns, and many times comes to agreement in Christ.

Think of the wide variety of perspectives found in your congregation and celebrate the diversity.

Are you comfortable being willing to think and let think?

God's Gracious Love

When John Wesley preached his message of God's salvation throughout England, many of the established church leaders found his message unsettling. Had not God chosen the king, elected the leaders of the nation, and blessed those persons with power, wealth, and authority? Why did Wesley use his prodigious knowledge and passion to speak to the poor and outcast?

Wesley understood firsthand God's grace. Like the younger

son in Jesus's parable, he, too, had wandered away from God but had been received back again, not once but time and time again. Wesley believed that if he had experienced God's grace, so could every other person. When Wesley sent his priests to the United States of America, he urged them to offer Christ to a people who had never heard the story of the prodigal son. Wesley was confident that when people experienced the fullness of God's grace, they would respond, their lives would change, and they would in turn change the world.

This practical theology of grace remains for United Methodist Christians today our most precious heritage. We listen for God and then respond. We discover that God is present with us at every moment of our lives, and God invites us to answer with our lips, our lives, and our service until "at the name of Jesus everyone in heaven, on earth, and under the earth might bow and every tongue confess that Jesus Christ is Lord, to the glory of God the Father" (Philippians 2:10-11).

Hymn Stanza

See how great a flame aspires,
	kindled by a spark of grace.
Jesus' love the nations fires,
	sets the kingdoms on a blaze.
To bring fire on earth he came,
	kindled in some hearts it is;
O that all might catch the flame,
	all partake the glorious bliss!

—Charles Wesley (*The United Methodist Hymnal*, 541)

Notes

1. *Discipline*, "Doctrinal Heritage" ¶ 102, "Doctrinal History" ¶ 103, "Doctrinal Standards" ¶ 104, and "Our Theological Task" ¶ 105.
2. *Works: Vol. 1*, p. 104.
3. *Works: Vol. 8*, "Large Minutes," p. 299; *Discipline*, ¶ 102, p. 51.

4. Langford, *Practical Divinity: Theology in the Wesleyan Tradition* (Abingdon: Nashville, 1983), p. 21.

5 *Works: Vol. 9*, "The Character of a Methodist," pp. 31-46.

6. *Discipline*, ¶ 102, pp. 51-54.

7. Langford, *Practical Divinity*, pp. 248-250. See also extended discussion about grace in the 1988 "Grace Upon Grace: The Mission Statement of The United Methodist Church" approved by the 1988 General Conference and the current extensive online commentaries on this mission statement: "Grace Upon Grace Commentary: A UM & Global Collection."

8. *Works: Vol. 2*, "The Scripture Way of Salvation" Sermon 43 (1769), pp. 153-169.

9. *Discipline*, "Inclusiveness of the Church" ¶ 4 Article IV; "Called to Inclusiveness" ¶ 140.

10 *Discipline*, ¶ 103, p. 56.

5. How Do United Methodists Nurture Our Spiritual Lives?

United Methodist Christians reveal God's grace by their inward piety.[1]

I [Paul] encourage you to live as people worthy of the call you received from God. Conduct yourselves with all humility, gentleness, and patience. Accept each other with love, and make an effort to preserve the unity of the Spirit with the peace that ties you together. You are one body and one spirit, just as God also called you in one hope. There is one Lord, one faith, one baptism, and one God and Father of all, who is over all, through all, and in all.

EPHESIANS 4:1-6

Personal Holiness and Social Holiness

How does God's grace reveal itself in our lives? United Methodist Christians are Bible Moths; we belong to the church universal; and we have our own rich history and grace-filled theology. How do we lead lives worthy of this heritage? As recipients of the love of God, United Methodists reveal God's grace through both personal and social holiness. We seek to maintain a balance between faith and works, belief and action, and inward piety and outward service.

When United Methodists go on mission trips to the Appalachian Mountains, inner-city missions, eastern Europe, western Africa, or Laos, we tell our faith stories and build social service centers. When United Methodists hear the voice of God, are forgiven and made right with God, gain the assurance that we are

God's children, and grow in our love for God and other people, we give evidence of this grace through both our acts of piety and works of mercy. In this chapter, we focus on individual and group spiritual disciplines. In the next chapter, we will turn to the good works we do.

Where do you find balance between faith and good works?

The General Rules

Inward piety and outward service are described in one of the most important documents in our United Methodist tradition: "The General Rules." When people began to gather around John Wesley to grow as followers of Jesus Christ, he created small groups for personal growth, mutual accountability, and spiritual direction as they observed three rules: do no harm, do good, and stay in love with God.

Wesley published "The General Rules" in a short pamphlet outlining his expectations of the Methodists. He republished this document more often than anything else he ever wrote. "The General Rules" are still found in our *Book of Discipline.*[2] To reveal God's grace at work in the lives of the Methodists, Wesley expected them to avoid evil, act righteously, and observe spiritual disciplines. These rules continue to serve as the rock-solid foundation for our denomination. These rules balance works of mercy with works of piety. While United Methodists engage in compassionate and just social action, we also spend time in personal and corporate prayer, Bible study, and worship.

What are the rules you follow in your life?

Classes and Small Groups

The success of the Methodist movement rested on Wesley's practical method of empowering people to help each other become serious disciples of Jesus Christ. Wesley established small neighborhood groups called classes. The typical class consisted of twelve persons including men and women. They met in members' homes, shops, or schoolrooms for an hour or two each week.

The class leader, a layman or laywoman chosen on the basis of spiritual maturity, held each class together. Each class meeting began with an opening hymn and the reading of the three rules. One by one, the members would then report on their success or lack of progress in living a grace-filled life. In response to the first rule to do no harm, persons might report that throughout the previous week they had avoided strong drink or refused to gossip. When asked about doing good, members might reply that they had visited the prison or taken food to a hungry neighbor. Finally, in their report on the third rule to keep spiritual disciplines, class members might share that they had attended worship on Sunday and prayed every day. Wesley understood the power of balancing large gatherings for worship with small groups for personal accountability and growth. As he wrote, these small groups were "no other than a company of [people] having the *form* and seeking the *power* of godliness, united in order to pray together, to receive the word of exhortation, and

81

to watch over one another in love, that they may help each other to work out their salvation."[3]

Today many United Methodists still experience the power of small groups for Christian formation. While worship brings a congregation together for prayer, praise, and edification, only in small groups do skillful leaders and other members challenge us on a personal level. In covenant discipleship groups, Sunday school classes, and other small gatherings, United Methodists meet regularly to hold one another accountable for spiritual growth.

United Methodist camps and retreat centers around the world provide wonderful settings for persons of all ages to gather for spiritual formation through small groups, fellowship, recreation, and worship. For over a century, United Methodists have stayed in love with God at historic centers such as Chautauqua in upper New York and Lake Junaluska in the mountains of North Carolina. Ann's youth group grew in their relationship with God and one another one weekend by the beautiful waters of Lake Tahoe United Methodist Retreat Center in California.

Do you belong to a small group that keeps you accountable for your salvation? Where do you go for spiritual nourishment?

Observing Spiritual Disciplines

We will return to the first two rules—doing good and avoiding evil—in the next chapter. Here we focus on the third rule, instructing people to observe "the public worship of God; the ministry of the Word either read or expounded; the Supper of the Lord; family and private prayer; searching the Scriptures; and fasting or abstinence."[4]

Wesley called these spiritual disciplines "means of grace." These religious practices are the channels or paths through which God's grace is received. The full riches of God's grace are poured out when Christians gather with others to worship, hear the Scriptures read and interpreted, share the bread and cup of Holy Communion, participate in a service of baptism, offer prayers for themselves and others, and observe a fast. As Wesley said, "By 'means of grace' I understand outward signs, words, or actions, ordained of God, and appointed for this end, to be the ordinary channels whereby God might convey to men [and women], preventing, justifying, or sanctifying grace." Even more pointedly, he claimed that "There is but one scriptural way wherein we receive inward grace—through the outward means which God hath ordained."[5]

Wesley described one person coming to a new relationship with God using these spiritual disciplines. To paraphrase Wesley, a woman may be living her life totally unaware of God, but then she receives a nudge from God during a conversation or in the midst of a life transition. In response, she draws closer to God by attending worship and reading the Bible. The more she ponders and prays, the more she is convinced of the love of God. She comes to worship, receives Holy Communion, reads the Bible, and prays until God speaks to her heart, "Your faith has saved you. Go in peace."[6] The whole journey of salvation takes place in the intersection of God's grace and human faith, as experienced in these devotional pathways.

United Methodists continue to grow in faith through the means of grace. We read the Bible and pray. We participate in small groups, which embrace us and hold us accountable. On Sundays and other days of the week, people gather for worship. We watch a child being baptized and everyone come to the table for Holy Communion. One such holy moment in Andy's congregation occurred when Pastor Reta, who had been diagnosed with cancer, knelt down for the children to lay hands on her and pray for healing. Such expressions of faith happen regularly in every United Methodist congregation.

How have these means of grace accompanied you in your journey of faith?

Individual Acts of Piety: Bible Study, Prayer, and Fasting

United Methodists stay in love with God through the practice of basic spiritual disciplines in our own daily lives. When we read and study the Bible, pray, and fast, we enter into deep communion with God. As discussed in the first chapter, United Methodists are people of the Bible. Our study of the Bible both privately and publicly enables us to listen to the voice of God. Our study of the Bible is the foundation of our spiritual lives.

Prayer is next. Jesus prayed morning, noon, and night. He prayed when alone and with other people, in public, and even on the cross. God is always accessible to people who pray or express to God their gratitude and need for help. The Bible instructs us to pray constantly (1 Thessalonians 5:17). We pray in the morning as we awake, when we hear about a natural disaster or a friend's personal crisis, before we make an important decision, at mealtime, with our children at bedtime, and before we close our eyes to sleep. Every occasion is a good time to pray. Prayer is sharing with God the most needful and happiest parts of our lives and then listening for God's response.

A variety of resources are available for guidance in Bible study and prayer. *The Upper Room*, a daily devotional guide created by Methodists in 1935, is today published in thirty languages in one hundred countries. The guide provides one verse of Scripture, a short devotion, and a prayer for the individual's devotional time. *The Upper Room Disciplines* is a more in-depth daily devotional guide. Each morning, Sally reflects on God's presence through an inspirational photograph posted online by the Upper Room. Each person can grow closer to God through prayer. As Protestant Christians, we affirm the priesthood of all believers. Everyone, not just our clergy, can be in immediate communication with God about our hopes and dreams, our needs and concerns. Because we are all priests, every Christian also has an obligation to pray for other people and for crisis situations. We find models of prayer throughout the Bible and Christian tradition. Our *United Methodist Book of Worship* is a helpful source of these prayers. Other prayers surface spontaneously out of our own needs and in our own words. During worship in many United Methodist congregations, we pray the Lord's Prayer, which was first taught by Jesus to his first disciples. As modern-day disciples, we continue to pray the Lord's Prayer in public worship, at funerals and weddings, and in private devotions. In all of our prayers, the greatest gift we receive is the gift of God's presence. Prayer assures us that we are not alone. Through prayer, we experience Jesus's presence in our lives, align our personal perspectives with God's perspective, and discern the next steps in our faith journeys.

In one of Andy's congregations, a remarkable group of women prayed every Wednesday. Six women, who said that they were too old to do anything else, came into the sanctuary, knelt at the prayer rail, and prayed by name for the sick and homebound, individuals with special needs, and each staff member. Next, the women touched the pulpit, the lectern, the baptismal font, the choir loft, the organ, and the piano, praying for the people who would be in those spots that coming Sunday. They then prayed at each pew for the people who would sit there. Finally, the women prayed at each doorway for the people who would enter the sanctuary that week. These faithful church women provided a powerful witness to the importance of prayer.

Fasting and abstinence, although not regularly practiced today by many United Methodists, is an additional act of personal piety. Wesley fasted at least twice every week by refusing to eat or drink anything other than hot tea before 3:00 o'clock in the afternoon. As he wrote: "Fasting is . . . a means in the hand of God, of confirming and increasing, not one virtue, . . . but also seriousness of spirit, earnestness, sensibility, and tenderness of conscience, deadness to the world, and consequently the love of God, and every holy and heavenly affection."[7]

We United Methodists may still fast or abstain from a particular food for spiritual growth. We might fast for a day or more during the season of Lent or give up one meal a day each week. Through the spiritual practice of fasting, we will discover our continuing need to be fed by God in our bodies and souls.

What are your practices of the study of the Bible, prayer, and fasting?

Community Acts of Piety: Worship and Preaching

The pathways to grace are not just personal and private but also communal. United Methodists always live connected to other Christians, both in our local congregations and with Christians around the world.

Worship is the most visible way that United Methodists stay connected. United Methodists follow the same Basic Pattern of Worship—Entrance, Proclamation and Praise, Thanksgiving and Communion, and Sending Forth—described in our *United Methodist Hymnal* and *United Methodist Book of Worship*. We come together, are attentive to the Word of God, respond by giving thanks and sharing the Lord's Supper, and then leave to serve the world.

While the pattern of worship is constant, a wide variety of styles of worship characterize our local congregations. United Methodists in Nigeria do not worship the same way as they do in France, Iowa, or Samoa. Congregations of different sizes, in different regions, of different racial and ethnic compositions, and with different local traditions worship in diverse ways. Yet behind all our expressions of worship there is a basic unity.

Methodists have never been bound to one age or tradition in their worship. In every era, worship styles change to better serve a new generation. Wesley initiated a liturgical revival by becoming a traveling evangelist. He preached to thousands of people outdoors, celebrated the sacraments in fields and prisons, allowed laity to speak, and encouraged extemporaneous prayer. He read formal prayers and also prayed as the Holy Spirit led him.

Significantly, John Wesley and his brother Charles encouraged people to sing their faith. The brothers replaced paid choirs of boys and men with congregational singing. In the first hundred years of the denomination, many Methodists owned both a Bible and a hymnal. The Wesleys understood that the finest musical instrument created by God was the human voice. Pianos, organs, and musical instruments (other than a tuning fork) were not allowed in Methodist sanctuaries until after the American Civil War. While United Methodists may enjoy great choral music, gifted musicians, and praise bands who lead us in worship, we are truly United Methodists when we open our mouths and sing.

The recent adoptions of online worship reflect this openness to change. In 2012, when Andy's congregation launched on Christmas Eve one of our denomination's first online congregations, the computer server crashed when over 2,000 people from a dozen countries joined us in just the first few minutes. When the world faced the COVID pandemic, many congregations began to worship and celebrate Holy Communion online. Congregations are encouraged to design worship to meet their own particular context and needs.

Ann's congregation in California worships in two services: a contemporary service with a band in the fellowship hall and a traditional service with an organ in the sanctuary. Both services are streamed to an almost equal number of persons who join in worship online. In its worship services, her congregation has read through the Bible in a year, followed the lectionary, heard a sermon series on politics and religion, and focused on the themes of this very book.

How do you describe the style of worship in your congregation? Can you detect the basic pattern of worship?

Holy Communion and Baptism

The sacraments of Holy Communion and baptism are our most significant corporate acts of piety. Through the waters of baptism and the bread and cup of Holy Communion, the worshipping community receives God's grace. Wesley believed that Holy Communion, which we sometimes call the Lord's Supper, the Eucharist, or the Holy Meal, was the essential act of worship, and he himself received Communion on average every four days. Wesley also offered the Lord's Supper out-of-doors to everyone who wanted to commune with Jesus Christ.

In the Holy Meal, we experience the living presence of Jesus Christ through key sign-acts.[8] We remember that Jesus took bread, blessed the bread and cup, broke the bread, and gave them to his disciples. Whenever we share the Lord's Supper, God also takes us, blesses us, breaks us, and gives us to the world. The Holy Meal reminds us of the Passover, Jesus's last supper in Holy Week, his sharing of a meal with his disciples on Easter Day, and God's promise to feast with us in the new creation. Many of our congregations celebrate the Eucharist weekly as the highlight of worship.

United Methodists practice open Communion. Everyone is invited to Christ's table; there are no restrictions because of a person's age, ability to reason, membership in a local congregation, or even baptismal status. Because we trust that the prevenient grace of God is already inviting persons to the table, we welcome the stranger, member, guest, saint, sinner, old, and young to the table of Jesus Christ. Our use of grape juice encourages children and persons struggling with alcoholism to join.

Another distinctive aspect of United Methodist worship is our understanding and practice of baptism.[9] Baptism was initiated by Jesus Christ as a symbol and pledge of God's love for us, forgives our sins, and incorporates us into the body of Christ. This sacrament proclaims our adoption by grace and our response of faith. Because baptism initiates us into Christ's universal church, United Methodists recognize all Christian baptisms as valid, including Sally's baptism by immersion in her childhood Baptist congregation.

United Methodists baptize using water, but persons have the choice of being baptized by sprinkling, pouring, or immersion. Each mode of baptism brings out rich and diverse symbolism around the death of our old selves and our new lives in Jesus Christ through the gift of the Holy Spirit. The three of us have baptized new followers of Christ beside small fonts, in a baptismal pool in a sanctuary, and in rivers, pools, and the ocean.

Because United Methodists believe in God's prevenient grace, our congregations celebrate the baptism of infants and children.

Nowhere does the New Testament or the early church record that Christian families delayed the baptism of their children until they could make their own profession of faith. Jesus's words, "Let the children come to me, do not hinder them" (see Matthew 19:14), is included in one of our baptismal services to remind us that our Lord has expressly given to little children a place among the people of God.[10] When Sally and Andy baptized our two daughters and four grandchildren—Roan, Emmalena, Evelyn, and Albert—as babies, our family and congregation professed that God's grace was already at work in the lives of these young children.

The salvation journey, of course, does not end with baptism. Infants and children who have been baptized are encouraged later to make vows of Christian discipleship and full membership in a service of confirmation. In addition, youth and adults who were baptized years earlier may reaffirm the Baptismal Covenant. On the first Sunday of the year or at other significant times, members of the congregation may be invited to reaffirm their baptismal vows by coming forward, touching baptismal waters, and marking themselves with water.

Followers of Jesus will always have fresh, new experiences of God's presence in their lives. Sometimes the experience is so life-changing that a person may ask to be baptized again. For United Methodists, re-baptism is not practiced. God's promises to us in our baptisms are steadfast. Once baptized, we have been initiated into Christ's body, the church, and are members of the family of God without question. Reaffirming our baptismal vows, however, is always appropriate. We can reaffirm our commitment to Christian discipleship anytime we witness a baptism or participate in a service of baptismal reaffirmation.

Reflect on how your congregation baptizes and shares Holy Communion.

Further Ways of Worship

How else do United Methodist Christians exhibit piety in communion with one another? We have services of Christian Marriage and Death and Resurrection. Many United Methodist congregations observe the Christian Year: Advent, Christmas, the Day of Epiphany, Ordinary Time, Lent, Easter, the Day of Pentecost, and Ordinary Time again. As we journey through the church year and Scripture, in services such as on the Baptism of the Lord, Ash Wednesday, and All Saints Day, we join with all the saints in drawing near to God. Congregations also occasionally celebrate services of healing, blessings of animals, love feasts, morning or evening prayer services, and many other services to reconnect us with God.

Which are your favorite services of worship in your congregation? What is your favorite Christian hymn or song?

Money and Stewardship

Our individual acts of piety include even more spiritual disciplines. United Methodists also have teachings about the use of money. As early Methodists practiced the three General Rules, they became diligent and frugal. When these Methodists focused on their spiritual growth by giving up drinking, gambling, and wasteful living, their wealth accumulated. How would they use their newfound resources?

Wesley created three additional rules for the use of money by Methodists: Earn all you can. Save all you can. Give all you can.[11] Earn all you can, the first rule, encourages people to use their time, energy, and resources to create better lives for themselves, their families, and other people. We work not to earn money or salvation but to be a blessing to others. Every job can be a noble vocation, and if pursued with diligence and discipline, the job offers rewards of many kinds including self-worth and financial gain. If people work smart and hard, they should be compensated fairly. United Methodists honor those among us who labor.

The second rule is to save all you can. Wesley did not call for Methodists to invest wisely and build large savings accounts. Instead, save all you can was Wesley's call to Methodists to live more simply. He warned the early Methodists against extravagance, opulence, and self-gratification. He listed superfluous expenses, which unfortunately most of us still have: excessive furniture, clothing, entertainment, and food. Faithful Christians cannot reconcile the accumulation of luxuries with the need to share with the poor. We do need to save for our families and times of economic uncertainty; but, for the sake of others, United Methodists are obligated to observe simple, green, and sustainable lifestyles.

Earning and saving money are not ends in themselves but instead are means for following Wesley's third rule: give all you can. Christians give to others not to earn God's love but to witness to God's generosity, which allows us to be generous with others. United Methodists give generously to the mission and ministries of our local congregations and support financially the work of the denomination both regionally and globally. When needs arise, United Methodists give even more. Through the United Methodist Committee on Relief, United Methodists provide the financial help needed when hurricanes and earthquakes strike across the world. In 2022, United Methodists gave over $6 billion to God through our denomination.

How does your financial stewardship compare to these three rules?

Personal Holiness Revisited

The apostle Paul challenged Christians "to live as people worthy of the call you received from God" (Ephesians 4:1). Wesley's

General Rules advocated inward disciplines of piety for all persons, including Bible study, prayer, worship, observance of the sacraments, and financial stewardship that we might be formed in the image of Christ. May all of us live such worthy lives.

Hymn Stanza
> Love divine, all loves excelling,
> > joy of heaven, to earth come down;
> fix in us thy humble dwelling;
> > all thy faithful mercies crown!
> Jesus, thou art all compassion,
> > pure, unbounded love thou art;
> visit us with thy salvation;
> > enter every trembling heart.

—Charles Wesley (*The United Methodist Hymnal*, 384)

Notes

1. *Works: Vol. 9, The Methodist Societies: History, Nature, and Design*, pp. 67-75.
2. *Discipline,* ¶ 104, pp. 77-80.
3. *Ibid.*, p. 78.
4. *Ibid.*, p. 80.
5. *Works, Vol. 1*, "The Means of Grace," Sermon 16 (1872), pp. 376-397.
6. *Ibid.*
7. *Works: Vol. 1*, Sermon 27, "Upon Our Lord's Sermon on the Mount," pp. 592-611.
8. *Book of Resolutions*, "This Holy Mystery," 8032, is a comprehensive statement about the meaning and practice of Holy Communion.
9. *Ibid.*, "By Water and the Spirit," 8031. This is a comprehensive statement about the meaning and practice of baptism.
10. *Book of Worship*, p. 103.
11. *Works: Vol. 2*, Sermon 50 "The Use of Money" (1760), pp. 263-280.

6. How Do United Methodists Serve God and Our Neighbor?

United Methodist Christians reveal God's grace with works of mercy by doing no harm and doing good.[1]

[Jesus said,] "Now when [the Son of Man] comes in his majesty and all his angels are with him, he will sit on his majestic throne. All the nations will be gathered in front of him. He will separate [the people] from each other. . . .

"Then the king will say to [the people] on his right, 'Come, you who will receive good things from my Father. Inherit the kingdom that was prepared for you before the world began. I was hungry and you gave me food to eat. I was thirsty and you gave me a drink. I was a stranger and you welcomed me. I was naked and you gave me clothes to wear. I was sick and you took care of me. I was in prison and you visited me.'

"Then those [people] who are righteous will reply to [the king], 'Lord, when did we see you hungry and feed you, or thirsty and give you a drink? When did we see you as a stranger and welcome you, or naked and give you clothes to wear? When did we see you sick or in prison and visit you?'

"Then the king will reply to them, 'I assure you that when you have done it for one of the least of these brothers and sisters of mine, you have done it for me.'"

MATTHEW 25:31-40

Social Holiness

United Methodist Christians balance their individual and corporate acts of piety with works of mercy. The private and group spiritual disciplines of Bible study, prayer, and worship draw us into a closer relationship with Jesus Christ, but these practices are incomplete without accompanying acts of service. Jesus healed the sick, fed the hungry, and worked among the poor. To follow Jesus, we must do the same. United Methodists believe that salvation includes a life-long commitment to serving God.

Jesus rejoices whenever followers engage in God's mission to redeem all creation. On our salvation journey, each of us has the holy responsibility to give shelter to the homeless, water to the thirsty, hospitality to the stranger, and support to the prisoner. We reflect God's grace to us not only by our warm hearts, but also by our willingness to lend a helping hand.

Expressions of acts of mercy are everywhere in The United Methodist Church. Acts of service have been a vital part of the congregations that Ann has served. These local churches sponsored a recovery program for persons with addictions, a community garden, a preschool, mission work teams in economically disadvantaged communities, and a free weekly Friday night supper and prayer service for anyone in the community.

In your life, is there a balance between your inward and outward journeys of faith?

The Wyandot Mission

One of Andy's treasured pictures is a framed copy of a lithograph entitled "The Wyandot Indian Mission." This lithograph depicts the story of John Stewart, an African American freeman who once lived "a drunken and dissolute life." In 1816, Stewart was on his way to end "his worthless existence," but en route he overheard a group of Methodists in worship. Stewart "heard the singing, hesitated, entered the church, and was gloriously converted." Following his conversion, Stewart felt God's call to share the gospel to the impoverished Wyandot Indians in Ohio. He ministered among the Wyandots by wearing the rough clothing of a freeman, binding his long hair in Wyandot fashion, and preaching in the Wyandot language. In 1819, Stewart's outreach inspired the organization of the Mission Board of the Methodist Episcopal Church.[2]

What missions to others do you most admire and support?

The First Two General Rules

John Wesley directed the early Methodists to respond to God's grace with two rules: Do no harm. Do good. These two rules continue to direct how United Methodists serve the world today. Wesley gave examples of behavior antithetical to the first rule of "doing no harm, by avoiding evil in every kind." According to Wesley,

such evil practices are taking of the name of God in vain, . . .

drunkenness, . . . the giving or taking things with interest, . . . doing to others, as we would not they should do unto us, . . . the putting on of gold or costly apparel, . . . and laying up treasures upon earth.[3]

These warnings to avoid evil are still valid today. United Methodists keep the first rule when we do not speak disrespectfully about God and other people, abuse drugs and alcohol, observe business practices that rob others, abuse the environment, treat others differently than we would want to be treated, flaunt material possessions, and hoard our wealth.

The second rule has an even larger impact on our United Methodist service to the world: "doing good . . . of every possible sort, and as far as is possible, to all people: . . . to their bodies, by giving food to the hungry, by clothing the naked, by visiting or helping them that are sick, or in prison; to their souls, by instructing, reproving, or exhorting all we have any intercourse with by doing good especially to them that are of the household of faith."[4] The early Methodists in England dramatically impacted the lives of other people by setting up credit unions, establishing clothing closets and health clinics, and leading protests against slavery. Their caring spirit grabbed people's attention. Neighbors were attracted to early Methodist Bible studies and worship because they had already witnessed the Methodists' acts of service. Similarly, the mission projects of United Methodists today such as stocking food banks and tutoring in schools are often entry points for new followers of Jesus.

How successful have you been this week in doing no harm and doing good?

Missional

In grateful response to what God has done, The United Methodist Church exists for mission as expressed in the Lord's Prayer: "Bring in your kingdom so that your will is done on earth as it's done in heaven" (see Matthew 6:10). "Mission is the action of the God of grace . . . also the church's grateful response to what God has done, is doing, and will do."[5] As Charles Wesley wrote: "O that the world might taste and see the riches of his grace! The arms of love that compass me would all the world embrace."[6]

In most United Methodist congregations, this missional ethos of service can be observed as soon as you walk in the front door. You might notice a shopping cart to collect health kits for a flood-ravaged area, a sign-up sheet for mission volunteers, or backpacks to be filled with food for local children. United Methodists are eager to serve people both near and far.

Sally remembers the excitement of church members in the Avery Parish in the North Carolina mountains to serve. These United Methodists in seven small congregations established the Reaching Avery Ministry's Rack, better known as the RAM's Rack, to provide for community needs. In its first year, the RAM's Rack provided food boxes and gently used clothing to almost 10 percent of the residents in that rural and economically challenged county. These same United Methodists also signed up for a CROP Walk for Hunger and trudged up and down mountain roads on behalf of hungry families on the other side of the world. Thirty years later, the RAM's Rack continues to serve.

Our United Methodist missions to the world include congregational initiatives, district projects, conference emphases, and global outreach. Sometimes Christians debate whether they should feed the hungry in their own town or care for the poor in a far-off land. For United Methodists, the answer is both. Each year over 125,000 Volunteers in Mission serve beyond their local congregations.

What is your congregation doing to serve others and make God's kingdom a reality?

Local, Regional, and Global

Our focus on social holiness and mission is evident in the organizational structure of The United Methodist Church. Religious institutions can become overly hierarchical, stifle innovation, and engage in institutional survival. Wesley witnessed that within the Church of England. Today The United Methodist Church as an institution is not without flaws and the need for reformation. Nevertheless, our denomination provides structure, leadership, and resources for extensive local and global outreach.

The organizational structure of The United Methodist Church enables us to avoid evil and do good both locally and across the globe. Our connectional system reflects our mission, based on Jesus's Great Commission in Matthew 28:16-20 "to make disciples of Jesus Christ for the transformation of the world."[7] We believe that the whole world is our parish. United Methodists can accomplish more for others when we serve together than any of us can achieve separately.

What is your reaction to organized religion? Have you seen religious institutions accomplish good things both near and far?

Local Congregations

The most basic connectional unit in our denomination for mission is the local congregation. For United Methodists, "the local church provides the most significant arena through which disciple-making occurs."[8] The four principal activities in a local congregation are to welcome new people, relate persons to God through worship, equip people for ministry through education and training, and send disciples of Christ out to serve. Each activity leads to the other, and the cycle of welcoming, relating, equipping, and sending out repeats and expands.

The United Methodist Church in the United States has over 26,000 local congregations, which are led by over 35,000 clergy serving over five million members. Outside the United States, there are over 12,000 congregations with almost seven million members. Our denomination is still adjusting to no longer being a U.S.A.-centric denomination, which sometimes treats others in colonialist ways, but instead listens to every voice from everywhere as we discover our mission future together.

Local congregations are led by elected Church Councils, along with committees such as Trustees (care for property),

Pastor/Staff-Parish Relations (personnel), Finance (money), and Missions (outreach). Andy and Sally celebrate that our younger daughter, Sarah, is an active lay leader in her local United Methodist congregation. Each year, a local Charge Conference chooses new leaders. Laity lead all these bodies. And through shared leadership and structure, our ability to serve thrives.

United Methodists, however, do not only honor and support those laypeople who work within the church but persons who also share the grace of God with people outside the walls of the institutions. God's work is not only done inside church buildings and institutions, but even more so in the broader communities where we live. When United Methodists in community settings serve meals, donate blood, lead other nonprofit organizations, counsel youth, support abused spouses, and care for the elderly, they are the hands and feet of Jesus through our denomination.

What do you appreciate about your local congregation?

Ordained Clergy

The early New Testament church set apart leaders with particular gifts and skills for preaching, teaching, and serving. The United Methodist Church continues this tradition. Some of our local church leaders are committed laypersons trained for caring ministries, preaching, and community development. These persons include certified lay servants, lay speakers, and lay missioners.[9] Deaconesses and Home Missioners are laypeople who are called by God to full-time vocations in ministries of love, justice, and service.[10]

In response to God's call and the affirmation of the church community, other persons offer themselves in leadership as ordained and licensed ministers.[11] There are about 45,000 such clergy. Their leadership duties include leading in prayer, worship, Christian formation, church administration, and service. Elders, deacons, and local pastors are ordained or licensed only after a careful and prayerful process of discernment and examination. Elders, deacons, and local pastors have differing leadership roles in the church, but they are all called to be mature and committed disciples of Jesus Christ.

Elders are called and set apart for the ministry of Word, Sacrament, Order, and Service. While most elders serve as the pastors of local congregations, other elders are appointed to teach in a university, serve as chaplains in the military or a hospital, or administer one of the structural units of our denomination, such as a district or annual conference. Like elders, local pastors are usually appointed to preach, lead worship, and administer the life of a local congregation, but licensed only to serve locally within one ministry.

Deacons are called and set apart for the ministry of Love, Justice, and Service. Deacons are often appointed to a particular role within a local church, such as minister of music, discipleship, or education. Deacons can also be appointed to serve within a social agency, hospital, or other setting beyond the local church.

A yearly highlight for elders, local pastors, and deacons is the yearly regional gathering of the annual conference. The annual conference is the basic body of our denomination where clergy hold their membership. Local pastors, deacons, elders, and laypersons gather for worship, fellowship, and education. The yearly gathering strengthens vital connections with one another and God. At the annual conference, the resident bishop also confirms clergy appointments for the coming year.

Our congregations are also served exceptionally well by lay staff members, including musicians, church administrators, children's and youth ministers, communications and technology specialists, parish nurses, nursery workers, and custodians. Clergy, staff, and laypersons work together to strengthen both personal and social holiness. And even broader, every member of every United Methodist congregation is expected to share their prayers, gifts, and service both within and beyond the congregation. To be a healthy body of Christ, everyone's gifts are needed to be engaged in God's mission to transform lives and the world.

Who are the people that lead your local congregation? What are their gifts?

Beyond the Local Congregation

United Methodists are also organized to avoid evil and do good beyond local congregations. Every local congregation is clustered with neighboring United Methodist churches in units called districts. Each district is led by a district superintendent, who is appointed by a bishop to support the pastors and local churches. In the Salisbury District, where Sally was appointed as a district superintendent, the local churches partnered in Latino ministries, building projects, new church starts, unemployment response ministries, and ministries with people experiencing homelessness. Throughout the United States, local congregations are divided into about 500 districts.

Each district belongs to a larger regional unit called an annual conference. Our own Western North Carolina Annual Conference has eight districts. Bishops, who are elders and have been elected by clergy and laity at five jurisdictional conferences (made up of several annual conferences), are assigned to oversee the work of the clergy and local congregations. There are now 54 annual conferences in the United States and 80 outside the United States.

United Methodists in each annual conference join together in ministry and mission outreach. Annual conferences sponsor new congregations, provide health insurance for clergy, support United Methodist colleges and retirement homes, build homes for persons with intellectual and developmental disabilities, manage monies, and organize mission teams to serve throughout the world. Across the globe, United Methodist Christians support almost 300 retirement homes and long-term care facilities, over 80 hospitals, and over 500 community-care ministries.

On a global level, United Methodists have thirteen general agencies, councils, and commissions that coordinate and guide our mission. The United Methodist Church has no central church headquarters. Instead, the denominational agencies are located in several locations, including Washington, D.C. and Nashville, Tennessee. Our offices in the District of Columbia are located next door to the United States Supreme Court. Together these agencies manage our global finances, care for pensions, manage trusts and endowments, send forth missionaries, design hymnals, lobby politicians, prepare Bible studies, involve men and women in ministry, preserve our history, and advocate for women and our diverse racial and ethnic communities. These bodies are led by boards that include bishops, clergy, and laity from around the world.

Our denomination as a whole also responds to natural disasters throughout the world, supports thirteen seminaries in the United States, Africa University in Zimbabwe, The United Methodist University of Liberia, and contributes to eleven historically Black colleges in the United States. The local churches, districts, annual conferences, and general agencies work together to serve the world.

How well does this system work? Vital signs are everywhere. In 2010, The United Methodist Church opened autonomous Methodist congregations in Cambodia, Laos, and Thailand. In 2023, the United Methodist bishop from Mozambique established the first United Methodist congregation in Madagascar and participated in the baptism of 93 children and adults.[12] The first United Methodist pastors have been assigned to the predominantly Muslim nation of Tunisia in North Africa.[13] United Methodists are simply continuing the movement Wesley began two hundred years ago.

What is your perspective about The United Methodist Church beyond your local congregation?

Connectional

United Methodists call the relationship between all these persons and organizations connectionalism.[14] Our "connectional system expresses our missional life; it ties us together from local church to world church; it joins laity and clergy; and it holds a clergy in covenant."[15]

Our connection is neither top down from the general church to local congregations nor bottom up from local congregations to the global denomination, but our connection is an ongoing dialogue between every part to foster works of compassion and service. Pastors and laypeople from local congregations serve on all the boards and agencies of our church, and the boards and agencies assist local congregations in their mission. Everyone is accountable to everybody else. When you join one United Methodist congregation, you become a member of the entire connection.

Our connectionalism is expressed in our method for sharing money. When United Methodists earn all they can, save all they can, how do they give all they can? Where does the money placed in the offering plate at your local church go within this connectional system? Around 90 percent of all the money given stays in the local congregation, where the gifts pay salaries, provide maintenance, and support local programs and missions. Then, about 8 percent goes to the district and annual conference for ministerial expenses and regional missions, while 2 percent supports national and international agencies and missions. These denominational missions beyond the local level are supported through "apportionments" or "fair-share askings" or "tithes," which have been equitably allocated to local congregations based on their ability to give. In addition, most congregations participate in denominational special offerings for particular needs, such as disaster or hunger relief.

Another example of how our connectional system works is seen in the way the denomination holds title to real property. The titles for all local and denominational property and church buildings are held in trust for The United Methodist Church.[16] Begun by Wesley, this model ensures that each part of our connection perpetuates United Methodist doctrine and practice for the sake of the whole. The property of each local church and our other units are dedicated for ministry that extends the mission of the whole denomination. Our property must be used in ways that is consistent with *The Book of Discipline* of the denomination.

What do you know about your district or annual conference?

The Global Connection

Our United Methodist Church has even more organization beyond our local and regional institutions. Similar to the United States government, The United Methodist Church has three basic branches of governance: a Council of Bishops (administration), a Judicial Council (judicial), and a General Conference (legislative). While The United Methodist Church does not have a clear administrative branch, the Council of Bishops, with 66 active bishops (46 in the United States and 20 outside), provides general oversight to the denomination. The Judicial Council, which is composed of nine persons, resolves legal differences within the denomination.

The General Conference, which gathers every four years for two weeks, serves as the legislative branch of the denomination. Around eight hundred lay and clergy delegates from around the world write legislation for *The Book of Discipline*, which serves as our official book of doctrine, procedures, and laws. At General Conferences, delegates often have intense struggles with the shape of our denominational structure, mission priorities, requirements for ordination, budgets, statements about social issues, and more. The goal of the General Conference quadrennial meetings is to seek to perfect our denomination for the sake of our mission; thus, changes always occur.

Reflecting our global nature, more than one hundred language interpreters are present at the General Conference to translate the actions of the delegates into at least ten different languages in real time. The General Conference is the only body to speak for the entire denomination. In 2024, our General Conference will debate and revise our positions on human sexuality, the organization of our global church, the denomination's budget, a new set of social principles, and more. No one can ever predict how General Conference will act.

The United Methodist connectional system is generally effective. Thanks to the United Methodist Committee on Relief, United Methodists are among the first to respond quickly when disaster strikes. Because UMCOR's administrative costs are covered in the general church budget, it uses

100 percent of the money collected from special offerings for relief work. Whether it is an earthquake in Haiti, tornadoes in the Midwest, a hurricane in the Gulf of Mexico, or flooding in Pakistan, United Methodists show up to serve. UMCOR also assists persons affected by war and conflict. When Russian forces invaded Ukraine, UMCOR responded quickly to provide food, water, shelter, and medical supplies for displaced families in Ukraine, as well as refugees in Hungary, Poland, and Romania.

Additionally, the global ministries of our denomination work toward global health, environmental sustainability, and economic development. The Yambasu Agricultural Initiative in Benin, West Africa, includes a sustainable farming facility supported by fifteen annual conferences. Since 2017, United Methodists have invested more than $26 million in fifty countries to reach one million children and adolescents with life-saving health interventions. The mission outreach of United Methodists is impressive but not surprising.

You can learn more about our connectional system and how it leads us in service through the website for the denomination: www.umc.org. This site is the portal to thousands of other sites that provide information about every aspect of The United Methodist Church.

Have you ever checked out our United Methodist website?

The Social Principles

For United Methodists, doing no harm and doing good has widespread social implications. We believe that it is impossible to put God's love into action without getting involved in political and social arenas. In 2020, the Social Principles of The United Methodist Church were thoroughly rewritten to reflect more clearly the global nature and interests of our denomination. These Social Principles are not church law but reflect a thoughtful and prayerful response to the needs of the world.

While we share with other Christians basic affirmations of faith such as the Apostles' Creed, The United Methodist Social Creed is uniquely ours. Since 1908, Methodists have crafted creeds that address social issues. The Social Creed reads:

We believe in God, Creator of the world; and in Jesus Christ, the Redeemer of creation. We believe in the Holy Spirit, through whom we acknowledge God's gifts, and we repent of our sin in misusing these gifts to idolatrous ends.

We affirm the natural world as God's handiwork and dedicate ourselves to its preservation, enhancement, and faithful use by humankind.

We joyfully receive for ourselves and others the blessings of community, sexuality, marriage, and the family.

We commit ourselves to the rights of men, women, children, youth, young adults, the aging, and people with disabilities; to improvement of the quality of life; and to the rights and dignity of all persons.

We believe in the right and duty of persons to work for the glory of God and the good of themselves and others and in the protection of their welfare in so doing; in the rights to property as a trust from God, collective bargaining, and responsible consumption; and in the elimination of economic and social distress.

We dedicate ourselves to peace throughout the world, to the rule of justice and law among nations, and to individual freedom for all people of the world.

We believe in the present and final triumph of God's Word in human affairs and gladly accept our commission to manifest the life of the gospel in the world. Amen.[17]

The Social Principles and Social Creed offer a vision of the new creation God has called us to make visible and real. Because of our allegiance to these affirmations, General Conference revises every four years *The United Methodist Book of Resolutions*, which "state[s] the policy of The United Methodist Church on many current social issues and concerns."[18] United Methodists take stands on issues from sex trafficking to global warming to stem-cell research to national health care.

What is your response to "The Social Creed"?

Living in a Multi-Religious World

United Methodists also recognize that we serve God in a world surrounded by persons of many other religious traditions. Some countries where United Methodists live are predominantly Christian, yet others are predominantly Muslim or Hindu. How do we avoid evil and do good alongside persons who are Jewish, Islamic, Hindu, and other religious traditions? Religious tensions increasingly explode in violence and hatred. Much of the world's poverty, oppression, and warfare originate in religious struggles.

As followers of Jesus, we seek to be both neighbors and witnesses.[19] First, we honor people who follow other religious traditions as individuals created in the image of God. Jesus reminded the Jews of the inherent value of the Samaritans and shared his blessings with the Syrophoenician woman. United Methodists must meet, know, respect, and honor others, especially those persons who seem most alien to us. Second, United Methodists are called to share our witness that Jesus Christ is our Savior and the Savior of all creation. Through our words and deeds, United Methodists share God's grace and invite others to follow Jesus with us.

The first Jewish Bar Mitzvah in Cabarrus County, North Carolina, where Andy served, was in the fellowship hall of Central United Methodist Church. In nearby Charlotte, Andy and daughter Sarah attended a Passover Seder at the local Jewish synagogue, where a friend served as rabbi. Such experiences are common among United Methodists.

Throughout its history, The United Methodist Church has celebrated its mission to be neighbors and witnesses to many different people, including Koreans, Macedonians, Liberians, Hmong, and Puerto Ricans. Increasingly and blessedly, United Methodists from those cultures now are coming to the United States to be neighbors and witnesses to a wide variety of American cultures. When a Korean United Methodist pastor is appointed to a predominantly Anglo congregation in the United States, blessings can abound for everyone.

How is your own community becoming more religiously and culturally diverse?

Social Holiness Revisited

This chapter has covered a broad range of issues from individual acts of compassion to global efforts to continue God's grace-filled mission to all people and all creation. Wesley's instructions to do no harm and do good are still followed by United Methodist clergy and laity today in local, regional, and global efforts. As an extension of Jesus's ministry to preach good news to the poor, release to the captives, and recovery of sight to the blind, The United Methodist Church continues to make the entire world our place of outward service so that one day, by God's grace, love and justice will be known by all and God's kingdom will come on earth.

Hymn Stanza

Forth in thy name, O Lord, I go,
  my daily labor to pursue;
thee, only thee, resolved to know
  in all I think or speak or do.

—Charles Wesley (*The United Methodist Hymnal*, 438)

Notes

1. *Works: Vol. 9, The Methodist Societies: History, Nature, and Design,* pp. 67-75.
2. Quotations attached to the lithograph from a 1918 newspaper article, which said that at that time this was the most reproduced painting in the United States.
3. *Works: Vol. 9,* "The General Rules of the United Societies," pp. 67-76; *Discipline,* ¶ 104, pp. 78-79.
4. *Ibid.*
5. Langford, *Grace Upon Grace,* p. 4
6. "Jesus! the Name High over All," *The United Methodist Hymnal,* 193.
7. *Ibid.,* ¶ 120.
8. *Ibid.,* ¶¶ 201-269.
9. *Ibid.,* ¶¶ 266-269.
10. *Ibid.,* ¶ 1913.
11. *Ibid.,* ¶¶ 301-369.

12. *UM News,* https://www.umnews.org/en/category/church-growth, 4/24/2023.

13. *Ibid.,* 5/2/2023.

14. *Discipline,* ¶ 132.

15. Langford, *Grace Upon Grace,* p. 36.

16. *Discipline,* ¶¶ 2502-2504.

17. *Ibid.,* ¶ 166.

18. *Book of Resolutions,* p. 5.

19. *Ibid.,* "Called to be Neighbors and Witnesses," 3291-3293.

INVITATION TO BE A UNITED METHODIST CHRISTIAN

As we conclude this broad overview of The United Methodist Church, we now invite you to live as a United Methodist Christian. In our journeys of salvation, all of us need to recommit again and again to read our Bibles, be part of the universal church, celebrate our history, affirm our distinctive theological emphases—especially grace—and finally do no harm, do good, and observe spiritual disciplines in the midst of connectional believers.

You may have been United Methodist all of your life and are now even more convinced that you are in the right denomination. Or you may be exploring joining a local United Methodist congregation and believe that it is time to make a decision. Because United Methodists firmly believe in human free-will, how will you respond? What will you choose?

As parents, Ann and her husband, Nathan, are helping their children understand the importance of their choices. They often ask Roan and Emmalena to decide between making good choices and bad choices. Giving them the freedom and responsibility to choose has increased their children's maturity. Again, what will you choose?

In 1745, John Wesley challenged the first Methodists to choose wisely in his pamphlet "Advice to a People Called Methodist."[1] He began, "By Methodists I mean a people who profess to pursue . . . holiness of heart and life, inward and outward conformity in all things to the revealed will of God; . . . a steady imitation of God they worship . . . ; more particularly, in justice, mercy, and truth, or universal love filling the heart, and governing the life."[2] Wesley then reminded the Methodists:

1. You are a new people. . . .
2. Do not imagine that you can avoid giving offense. . . .
3. Trust God with your all, then go on with the power of [God's] might . . .
4. Be true to your principles.[3]

For the next forty years, the English and American Methodists strived to follow Wesley's advice to grow as faithful disciples of Jesus Christ. But ten years before his death, Wesley visited Methodists across Great Britain. He returned to London discouraged. Wesley wrote, "I am not afraid that Methodists should ever cease to exist. . . . But I am afraid, lest the Methodists should only exist as a dead denomination, having the form of religion without the power."[4]

When Wesley wrote these words, the Methodist movement was strong. There were 60,000 Methodists in England. The first Methodist denomination had just been formed in the United States of America. In the years to come, The United Methodist Church would be created. How would Wesley judge his heirs today?

Today, United Methodists remain recipients of God's love through Jesus Christ. Within local congregations and throughout the world, United Methodists still respond to God's grace and reaffirm our commitment to love God and our neighbors. We still go forth to serve and transform our communities and world. Although we United Methodists have often made mistakes, we believe that Wesley would be proud of his heirs.

As our bishops wrote:

> Christ's prayer for our unity and command to gather all to the table, to make space for one another, appreciate one another, and look for Christ in each other, prohibit us from creating individual tables only for those who think, act, look, and perceive the world like we do. . . .
>
> We cannot be a traditional church or a progressive church or a centrist church. We cannot be a gay or straight church. Our churches must be more than echo chambers made in our own image arguing with each other while neglecting our central purpose. . . .

Instead, we must be one people, rooted in scripture, centered in Christ, serving in love and united in the essentials. It is hard work. It is sacred work. It is the ministry of reconciliation that Christ gave to each of us. Our best witness is to love each other as Christ loves us, to show the world the supernatural power of the Holy Spirit to bind us together despite our differences. This is living out the gospel.[5]

Amen.

Notes

1. *Works: Vol. 9*, pp. 123-131.
2. *Ibid.*
3. *Ibid.*
4. *Ibid.,* "Thoughts Upon Methodism" (August 4, 1786), pp. 527-530.
5. "A Narrative for the Continuing United Methodist Church," November 2021.

UNITED METHODIST MEMBERSHIP VOWS

If you would like to join a local United Methodist congregation, you may do so in one of several ways:[1]

1. By Profession of Faith and Baptism. If you are not yet a baptized Christian, discuss with your pastor the meaning of baptism and church membership and continue your spiritual journey among the people called United Methodist.

2. By Transfer from Another Christian Denomination. If you have previously been part of another denomination, we would welcome you as a United Methodist. Your new congregation will write for your letter of membership at your former congregation. Because you have already been baptized, baptism will not be repeated.

3. By Transfer from Another United Methodist Congregation. If you wish to serve God in a new United Methodist congregation, your new church will request your letter of membership.

When joining The United Methodist Church, individuals are asked the fundamental question asked of all Christians:

Do you confess Jesus Christ as your Savior,
put your whole trust in his grace,
and promise to serve him as your Lord,
in union with the church, which Christ has opened
to people of all ages, nations, and races?[2]

Then, to be a United Methodist Christian, persons are asked two questions:

> As members of Christ's universal church,
> will you be loyal to The United Methodist Church,
> and do all in your power to strengthen its ministries?
> **I will.**

> As members of this congregation,
> will you faithfully participate in its ministries
> by your prayers, your presence, your gifts, your service,
> and your witness?
> **I will.**[3]

Are you willing and able to make these vows? What do you choose?

A Covenant Prayer in the Wesleyan Tradition

In 1755, Wesley celebrated the first Covenant Service in the Methodist movement. He celebrated the service at least once each year in clustered gatherings of his small groups as a way to remind all members of their commitment to God. Wesley claimed, "It was an occasion for a variety of spiritual experiences . . . I do not know that ever we had a greater blessing. Afterwards many desired to return thanks, either for a sense of pardon, for full salvation, or for a fresh manifestation of His graces, healing all their backslidings."[4]

The heart of the service was the Covenant Prayer. The following "Covenant Prayer in the Wesleyan Tradition" is an adaptation of Wesley's original prayer.[5] This prayer of commitment is our invitation to you to continue your journey as a United Methodist Christian:

> I am no longer my own, but thine.
> Put me to what thou wilt, rank me with whom thou wilt.
> Put me to doing, put me to suffering.

Let me be employed by thee or laid aside for thee,
   exalted for thee or brought low by thee.
Let me be full, let me be empty.
Let me have all things, let me have nothing.
I freely and heartily yield all things
   to thy pleasure and disposal.
And now, O glorious and blessed God,
   Father, Son, and Holy Spirit,
    thou art mine, and I am thine. So be it.
And the covenant which I have made on earth,
   let it be ratified in heaven.

Let all United Methodists reclaim who we are, revive our spirits, and renew this wonderful communion.

Amen. And Amen.

Notes

1. Details about membership in The United Methodist Church are found in the *Discipline*, ¶¶ 214-242.
2. *The United Methodist Hymnal*, 34.
3. *Ibid.*, 38, revised by the 2008 General Conference to include "witness."
4. *Book of Worship*, 288.
5. *The United Methodist Hymnal*, 607.

IF YOU WANT TO KNOW MORE

The following resources will help you study further The United Methodist Church and what it means to be a United Methodist Christian.

Official Resources

The following may be found in print and electronically:

The Book of Discipline of The United Methodist Church. Nashville: The United Methodist Publishing House, 2016. The *Discipline* contains the official beliefs, policies, and rules of organization approved by The United Methodist General Conference. The *Discipline* will be revised in 2024.

The Book of Resolutions of The United Methodist Church. Nashville: The United Methodist Publishing House, 2016. The *Book of Resolutions*, approved by The United Methodist General Conference, details United Methodist perspectives on many personal, national, and global issues. The *Book of Resolutions* will be revised in 2024.

The United Methodist Hymnal. Nashville: The United Methodist Publishing House, 1989. The official songbook of our denomination that also includes our basic services of worship.

Other official United Methodist hymnals and books of worship include: *Mil Voces Para Celebrar: Himnario Metodista* (1996) and *Come, Let Us Worship: The Korean-English United Methodist*

Hymnal (2000), plus other supplemental hymnals, songbooks, and worship resources.

The United Methodist Book of Worship. Nashville: The United Methodist Publishing House, 1992. This resource contains the official liturgies of our denomination including Services of Word and Table, Services of Baptism, the Revised Common Lectionary, prayers, special acts of worship, and more.

The Works of John Wesley. Nashville: Abingdon. Begun in 1960, this is the definitive collection of Wesley's writing with scholarly notes. To date 23 of the total 35 volumes have been published.

Helpful Link

The official website of The United Methodist Church is www.umc.org. This website offers links to United Methodist congregations, districts, annual conferences, general agencies, and more, with information about many facets of our denomination.

BIBLIOGRAPHY

Bickerton, Tom. "Reclaim. Revive. Renew.: Mid-Term State of The United Methodist Church Address," March 2, 2023; https://www.umc.org/en/content/reclaim-revive-renew-the-necessity-of-union-among-us.

Book of Discipline of The United Methodist Church, The. Nashville: The United Methodist Publishing House, 2016.

Book of Resolutions of The United Methodist Church, The. Nashville: The United Methodist Publishing House, 2016.

Council of Bishops, The United Methodist Church. "A Narrative for the Continuing United Methodist Church," November 2021; https://www.unitedmethodistbishops.org/files/websites/www/a+narrative+for+the+continuing+united+methodist+church....._.pdf.

Croft, Stephen, editor. *Mission-Shaped Questions: Defining Issues for Today's Church.* New York: Seabury Books, 2010.

Edwards, Luke. *Becoming Church: A Trail Guide for Starting Fresh Expressions.* 2021. Available at at https://freshexpressions.com.

_____. *How to Start a New Kind of Church.* ebook, 2023. Available at https://freshexpressions.com/howtostart.

Jones, L. Gregory, Robert Johnston, Jonathan Wilson. *Grace Upon Grace: Essays in Honor of Thomas A. Langford.* Nashville: Abingdon Press, 1999.

Keillor, Garrison. "Those People called Methodists"; https://www.beliefnet.com/columnists/bibleandculture/2007/02/garrison-keillor-on-those-people-called-methodists.html.

Langford, Thomas A., editor. *Doctrine and Theology in The United Methodist Church.* Nashville: Abingdon Press, 1991.

_____. *God Made Known.* Nashville: Abingdon Press, 1992.

_____. *Grace upon Grace: The Mission Statement of The United Methodist Church.* Nashville: Graded Press, 1990.

_____. *Practical Divinity: Theology in the Wesleyan Tradition.* Nashville: Abingdon Press, 1983; revised into two volumes in 1984.

_____. *Wesleyan Theology: A Sourcebook.* Labyrinth, 1984.

UM News, https://www.umnews.org.

United Methodist Book of Worship, The. Nashville: The United Methodist Publishing House, 1992.

United Methodist Hymnal, The. Nashville: The United Methodist Publishing House, 1989.

Wesley, John. John Wesley's "Preface to Explanatory Notes upon the Old Testament," first published in Edinburgh, April 25, 1765; https://www.swartzentrover.com/cotor/E-Books/BookScans/Wesley%20-%20John%20Wesley's%20Notes%20-%20The%20Old%20Testament.pdf.

Willimon, *Will. Don't Look Back: Methodist Hope for What Comes Next.* Nashville: Abingdon Press, 2022.

Works of John Wesley, The. Nashville: Abingdon. Begun in 1960, this is the definitive collection of Wesley's writing with scholarly notes. To date, 23 of the total 35 volumes have been published.

ABOUT THE AUTHORS

Sally and Andy Langford are United Methodist pastors in North Carolina. Their daughter Ann Langford Duncan is a United Methodist pastor serving in California.

Andy's family have been Methodists for at least six generations, while Sally became United Methodist after college. Ann was born into this tradition.

Sally was educated at Converse College, Duke Divinity School, and Vanderbilt University. She has pastored in North Carolina, Georgia, and Tennessee, and served as an assistant to Bishop Larry Goodpaster and twice as a district superintendent. She taught United Methodist polity at Hood Theological Seminary. She was a delegate to three General Conferences. In 2011 she and Andy wrote *Living as United Methodist Christians: Our History, Our Beliefs, Our Practices* (Abingdon).

Andy graduated from Davidson College, Duke Divinity School, and Emory University. He worked on *The United Methodist Hymnal* committee; edited *The United Methodist Book of Worship*; directed worship, music, and preaching training and resources for all United Methodist congregations; and attended eight General Conferences either as staff or as a delegate. He also served for twelve years as a voting member on The General Council on Ministries/Connectional Table, the highest general agency in the denomination, which coordinates the work and budgets of the agencies that serve the worldwide United Methodist Church.

Ann, a former Peace Corps volunteer, is a graduate of Duke University and Boston University School of Theology. She has pastored in congregations in North Carolina and now serves a congregation in Burlingame, California. In 2012, she wrote with her father *The Gospel According to the Hunger Games Trilogy.*

They have all served in a wide variety of United Methodist congregations and on district, conference, jurisdictional, and global committees, and have written many other books and resources. This is their first book together.

Made in United States
Troutdale, OR
02/06/2024

17495289R00077